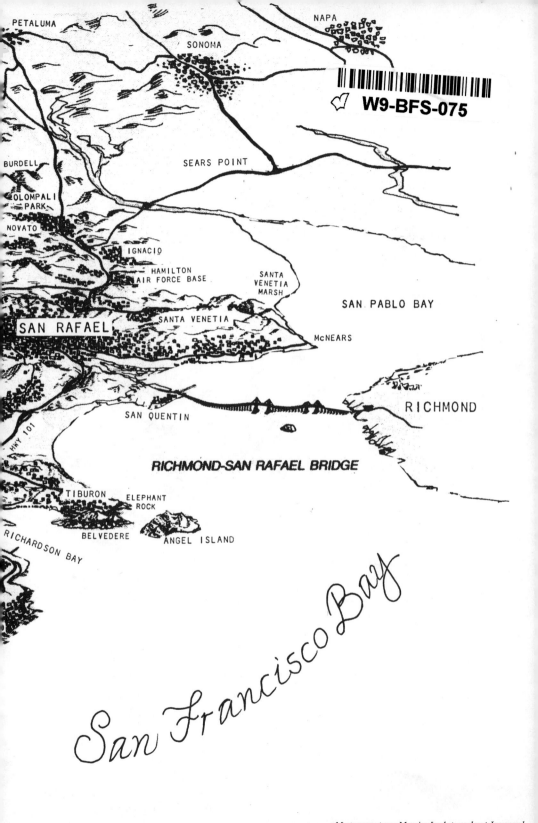

PETALUMA

NAPA

SONOMA

W9-BFS-075

SEARS POINT

BURDELL

OLOMPALI PARK

NOVATO

IGNACIO

HAMILTON AIR FORCE BASE

SANTA VENETIA MARSH

SAN PABLO BAY

SANTA VENETIA

SAN RAFAEL

McNEARS

RICHMOND

SAN QUENTIN

HWY 101

RICHMOND-SAN RAFAEL BRIDGE

TIBURON

ELEPHANT ROCK

BELVEDERE

ANGEL ISLAND

RICHARDSON BAY

San Francisco Bay

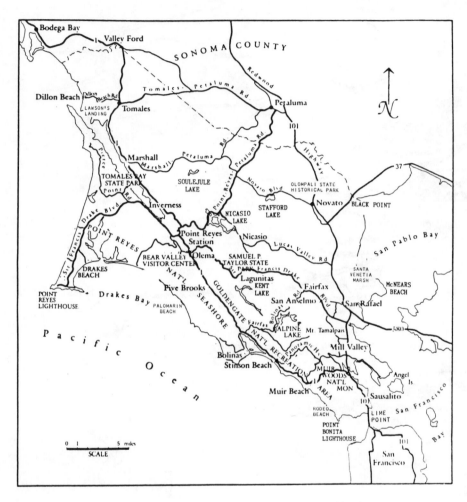

Map by Dewey Livingston

LIME POINT
TO LAWSON'S
LANDING

OUTDOORS IN MARIN

61 *MORE* PLACES TO VISIT
By DICK MURDOCK

Photographs & Captions
JAYNE MURDOCK

PREFACE: KENT DIEHL   **FOREWORD:** ANN WALSH

MAY -MURDOCK PUBLICATIONS   ROSS CALIFORNIA

Copyright © 1992 by Dick Murdock

FIRST PRINTING, January 1992

Some material in this book originally appeared
in the Marin Independent Journal
as outdoors columns by Dick Murdock
and are presented here with permission.

Library of Congress Catalog Card Number 91-20154
International Standard Book Number 0-932916-15-5

Library of Congress Cataloging-in-Publication Data

Murdock, Dick, 1917-
    Lime Point to Lawson's Landing : outdoors in Marin : 61 more places
to visit / by Dick Murdock : photographs & captions by Jayne Murdock :
preface, Kent Diehl : foreword, Ann Walsh.

        p. cm.
    Includes bibliographical references and index.
    ISBN 0-932916-15-5 (pbk. : alk. paper) $10.95
    1.Marin County (Calif.)—Description and travel—Guide-books.
2. Outdoor recreation-California—Marin County—Guide-books.
I. Title.
F868.M3M77 1992
917.94'620453—dc20   91-20154
                                                      CIP

Published by
MAY-MURDOCK PUBLICATIONS
Drawer 1346 - 90 Glenwood Avenue
Ross CA 94957-1346

Printed in the United States of America

DEDICATION

To three of the many whose
foresight & generosity, vision & vigor
saved so much of Marin for us
to treasure and enjoy

William Kent: 1864 - 1928
Caroline Livermore: 1883 - 1968
Clem Miller: 1916 - 1962

...lift up thine eyes and look
from the place where thou art —
northward, and southward, and
eastward, and westward...walk
in the land through its length
and width.

Genesis 13:14,17

Large oak, Santa Margarita Island

PREFACE

In 1937, it dawned on me Marin is a magical place. I was pulled from my parent's car, one of the first to cross the Golden Gate Bridge, to look back at the awesome scene of San Francisco across the Bay. Buildings, streets, scores of houses held my gaze, as it does to this day. But turn around and scramble to a high point and look north, west and east . . . then as now green or golden grass, undulating ridges bucking up Mount Tamalpais, bays and harbors.

There is some fencing now, homes and docks swelling to the great demand, but fly over this estate of God. You will gaze in disbelief at the wildness and solitude beneath you. Marin has very few key roads. Green miles are all around you in winter. Sun gilds all of this gold, turning the bleakest country into a captivating, spell binding wind-waved paradise. Reflected flashes tell you homes and cars are down there cutting through the lonely miles as infrequent reminders of habitation.

Ours is a land of pure air, Niagaras of fog roaring off Wolf Back Ridge, rocky streams, hidden waterfalls, beaches that flaunt precious and semi-precious stones, middens that mark the spot where the Miwoks, for a thousand years, worshipped the rising sun between the peaks of Mount Diablo across the bay, at the exact moment of the vernal equinox, a canyon where mountain lion, coyote, and ringtail cats live in the sweetness of the moss, Tiburon hillsides glorified by the fluttering flight of a now endangered butterfly, a hilltop where hawks by the thousands stop, rest and gather courage to cross the treacherous waters of the Golden Gate, lonely beaches where elephant seals mate and carpets of native California poppy roll up the hillsides into the fogs of utter solitude.

Incredible when a printed fertile source appears pinpointing glorious spots near at hand that I've never even heard of — Roy's Redwoods, Jake's Island, Chicken Ranch Beach. Really!!

Dick and Jayne Murdock's prolific wanderings have caught my attention and unending admiration, along with their writing, before. *Point Bonita to Point Reyes* had my Sheila and Keila accompanying me to innumerable valleys and beaches. We took up the search for the spot where Sir Francis Drake careened the Golden Hinde and have confronted the wind and tide to uncover relics at Agate Beach. Chilled, we retired to the warm hills above Tomales Bay to watch herds of Tule Elk rumble by, toasting them with a Marin Appellation wine.

Now the Murdocks have done it again — *Lime Point to Lawson's Landing.* Enjoy this wonderful volume. Irresistible unique Marin! Pick a page and go. The distant past will seem close at hand as you discover our ambiance with history. I'll say it again, "The Murdocks have chosen such special places around a county so beautiful, I've applied for another lifetime."

Although my great Arabian stallion, Shobatan, who showed me the way in the blackest of nights was tragically killed, my saddle is ready to be thrown on the next good horse for a visit to Roy's Redwoods, or whatever.

This enthralling Marin offers the richness of the world's very best. Yet everywhere are reminders that this fragile land, this wild beauty, the love affair with our environment could be erased.

Leave it better than you found it — Our Marin.

Kent B. Diehl
President, Board of Directors
Marin Cultural Center and Museum
April 1991

Muir Beack Overlook

viii

FOREWORD

In Manchester, England, where I am from, I have a 10 year old niece who wants desperately to follow in her Aunt Ann's footsteps and come to America. Little wonder. Each time I visit her there in gray, rainy Manchester, I tell her wonderful stories of life here in marvelous Marin — how I live on the edge of America, on the other side of the Golden Gate Bridge, in a fabled place filled with enterprising people and unsurpassed natural beauty.

"I live in God's Country," I tell my niece. Her eyes sparkle with wonder.

Now there's a marvelous new guide to God's Country — Dick Murdock's outstanding book, *Lime Point to Lawson's Landing: Outdoors in Marin, 61 MORE Places to Visit*. In these 160 pages you'll find a whole host of delightful diversions, seaside strolls and open-air outings in the Bay Area's most beautiful county.

It's a magnificent testament to our environment — and to people like Dick and Jayne Murdock, true stewards of our precious open space in Marin County.

The book lists 61 very special destinations. Thanks to Dick's hard work digging up information, his friendly, inviting style of writing, and wife Jayne's sensational photography, Marin County's natural treasures are now as accessible as reading a chapter of this beautifully designed book.

Have you ever strolled to Lime Point with the sea at your feet and the Golden Gate Bridge overhead? Or wandered past salt marshes and singing birds at Jake's Island? Or visited fascinating Olompali State Historical Park, where Coastal Miwok Indians once lived in great numbers?

The Murdocks have. In this book they'll take you there — and to quite a number of other spots as well. Some destinations, like Roy's Redwoods in the Nicasio Valley, are hidden treasures that only the most adventurous know by name. Others, like Old Mill Park in Mill Valley, are better known, but no less beautiful.

I'm familiar with Dick's wit and his ability to pen a friendly phrase that's full of facts. This ex-railroad engineer, fishing fanatic and outdoor enthusiast wrote a wonderful column on fishing for the 1991 edition of *The Best of Marin*. By all accounts, our readers like it as much as I do. That's why I'm so pleased to recommend *Lime Point to Lawson's Landing: Outdoors in Marin*.

For me — someone who has long supported protection of our open spaces and who enjoys getting away from crowds and hiking through verdant forests, enjoying nature in all its glory — the book is a perfect companion for a Sunday afternoon stroll. It's also a handsome companion to Dick's first volume, *Point Bonita to Point Reyes*, which won the prestigious Best Book Award for 1990 from the Outdoor Writers Association of California.

And *Lime Point to Lawson's Landing* couldn't have been published at a more opportune time. I recently got a call from Manchester. My niece announced that her dream is going to come true. She's coming to America. To visit God's Country. So you can be sure both of Dick's books will be close at hand.

Ann Walsh, Publisher
The Best of Marin
San Anselmo CA
April 1991

Schoonmaker Point Marina, Sausalito

INTRODUCTION

As this book comes together and is readied for printing, I am once again amazed at the process. Way back, almost on the heels of *Point Bonita to Point Reyes*, Dick and I decided to produce a second Marin outdoors book and to call it *Lime Point to Lawson's Landing*.

We started in the fall of 1989 to check Dick's Sunday columns, already run in the Independent Journal's "Marin at Play" feature (before the format was changed eliminating his Sunday contributions) to pick those we wanted to use, and to choose other spots around the county to research for inclusion in the projected book.

We were barely underway when began the series of events that led Dick to double bypass heart surgery at the end of March 1990.

The next time we looked around, the year was half over and we postponed the project.

So it was, while visiting my daughter for the birth of her fourth son in January 1991, I sorted out all we had previously done and all we planned to do, and made a calendar: So many places to visit each week, to write up and photograph, in black and white for the book, in slides for planned programs when the book came out.

Week after week, in January, through February, sometimes beautifully rained out in March, on into April, all the field work projected for completion before May 1.

We did it! And what a time we had. Marin County is so glorious, so diverse, so exciting! We climbed mountains, hiked trails, walked beaches, visited parks, marshlands, canyons, waterfalls. Each place was special.

I've lived in Marin for seventy years and was amazed, when we started *Point Bonita*, that there was so much I didn't know about this astounding county. We have now written the wonders of 122 different places. And guess what? There is more, much more. Enough for another book!

Gathering the material in the field, however, is the least of it. Dick writes the chapters soon as possible. Then it's editing, writing subtitles, captions for each picture. Checking, rechecking. Choosing the best photo is difficult. I wish we could use three for each place, not just one!

Tying all the loose ends together; foreword, preface, and the blurbs on the back cover, acknowledgements, indexing, dedication. The cover! A whole project in itself.

And then it's ready — ready for the typesetter, ready for the printer, ready for the color house, ready for delivery, ready for distributors, for book stores, for you!

We have a grand time producing these books on Marin. May you have a grand time reading — and using — them.

Jayne Murdock
Ross California
July 1991

Lime Point Lighthouse

CONTENTS

Restored 100-year old Dixie School House, Marinwood

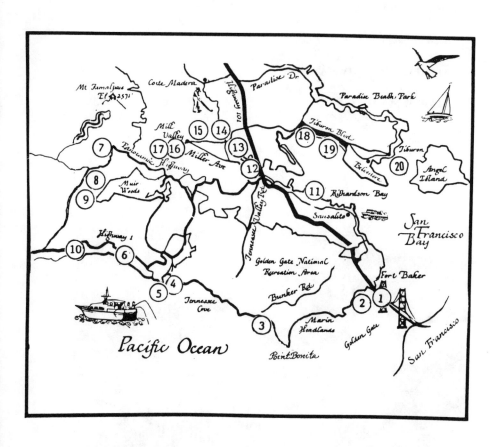

SOUTHERN MARIN

LIME POINT

bay at your feet, bridge overhead

PLENTY TO ENJOY here, all of it viewed while standing mere yards above sea level. On calm days, the ocean gently laps at your feet. Other times, breakers crash against gigantic nearby rocks. Nearly always a salt-tinged breeze, or stronger, will blow in your face.

A large gravelled parking lot is located almost directly beneath the north (Marin) portal of the Golden Gate Bridge. In fact, a fire road, above the parking area, circles the hill and leads back to Vista Point. If you want an exciting side trip, hike up this dirt road, enjoy the magnificent view, then take the walkway under the bridge to the trailhead parking lot and make your way on the paved road down to your car. Continue to your original destination, Lime Point.

A wide path (no bicycles, wheelchairs okay) leads southwest with a picnic table at the starting point and observation benches placed at intervals. The view of the San Francisco skyline is spectacular, tall buildings etching the horizon in impressive fashion. Light mist often adds an intriguing halo effect. When fog is heavy, with loud horns blaring raspy warnings, even the north tower directly overhead disappears into the wet gray above.

The walk to Lime Point beneath the bridge is not long, perhaps a quarter mile at best, some stretches protected from the sea by aged iron railings. Near what's left of the historic lighthouse structure, the walkway ends. Here you'll often find anglers shore-fishing from the limited space for perch, jacksmelt, rays, striped bass, an occasional salmon and rarely, a keeper sturgeon (44 inches or over).

18

Gulls wheel about, squawking for tidbits or loudly challenging your presence. Cormorants float in formation around Needle Rock, just off-shore. A locked iron gate prevents you from entering the old Lime Point structure, built 90 years ago, where the light still flashes, on duty at all times to warn of dangerous rocks nearby.

Amateur geologists will enjoy the leisurely walk to Lime Point and back and the amazing strata of steep cliffs leading above to where the rumble of bridge traffic sounds like an echo of the sea.

Fog obscures most of the Golden Gate Bridge and the San Francisco skyline. A lone car sits in the ample parking area. Needle Rock rises just offshore and the Lime Point structures jut into the bay below the cliff.

KIRBY COVE

2

down a dirt road to history

HAVE YOU EVER visited Kirby Cove off Conzelman Road just west of the Golden Gate Bridge's north portal?

If not, you're in for an invigorating and worthwhile outdoor experience. If so, you'll undoubtedly return. The iron gate is locked to cars except those with advance reservations for a camp site. The walk down the twisting smooth dirt road of less than a mile offers exciting views of the Pacific Ocean, Golden Gate Bridge and San Francisco skyline.

The bluffs are brushy at first but as the road decends pine trees appear. You'll see interesting shale formations in places where cuts in the road expose the strata on this easy downhill trek. While the headlands may be shrouded in fog, you soon drop below it as you approach pine, eucalyptus and cypress groves, entering the cove itself.

There's ample parking for those camping. Steps lead to four broad, clean camp areas with tent pads beneath a forest of stately pines. It's roomy, comfortable, well-kept, inviting. Restrooms are nearby, the camp host quarters just beyond. No RV or trailer camping allowed and no pets. Campers of 1 to 10 per site are by advance reservation only, with the Golden Gate National Recreation Area, phone 331-1540.

A broad loop circles historic Battery Kirby sitting on a knoll facing the Pacific, the old cement circular gun emplacement sites and square ammunition storage and generator rooms seemingly indestructible. Kids love to play and explore here, indeed a spot to bring young imaginations into full blossom.

0

The beach beyond is a 200-yard arc of fine brown sand separating a pair of jagged bluffs. Great views from here. Access is by stairs from either end. It looks like a fine place for surf fishing but not an angler in sight, only a group of children making sand castings under adult supervision. An old brick-lined drainage tunnel for the creek leads from the fort to the beach.

Leaving by the south trail you'll see a fine day-use picnic site. The path is bordered by sticky monkey plants with their orange flowers. Watch for wild cucumber vines climbing nearly to the crown of cypress trees.

Gentle waves lap the sandy beach. Framed by the Golden Gate Bridge, Alcatraz, the Bay Bridge and San Francisco's skyline are visible.

RODEO BEACH

3

calm lagoon, crashing surf, coarse sand

A S YOU HIKE, bike or drive to Rodeo (Cronkhite) Beach, take time to enjoy all you see en route, as you approach the World War II barracks. Be thankful that it is now part of the Golden Gate National Recreation Area and that the unscarred headlands in their rugged splendor remain untouched. It very nearly didn't stay this way.

In the mid-1960's, developer Thomas Frouge, backed by Gulf Oil, had big plans for a 30,000-population metropolis to be located here. He even installed a model of his dream city in a building in Sausalito. So impressive was his layout that the Board of Supervisors approved the plan.

As often happens after quick approvals, opposition rose immediately and the battle was on. Conservationists and the City of Sausalito disapproved. Then Frouge and Gulf Oil had differences leading to a three year legal battle. In January 1969, Frouge unexpectedly died, and the project, blessedly, died with him.

In the relocated visitor center in Ft. Barry's old chapel, Jayne and I found park ranger Gail Lester and her assistants most helpful, as always.

"Is the right name Rodeo or Cronkhite Beach?" I asked Gail.

"Rodeo," she replied. "It was called 'Rodeo' long before the military came and Fort Cronkhite was built."

After looking at the exhibits and books for sale, we drove on down the road to the parking spaces opposite the old army barracks. We left

22

the car and walked the wooden bridge spanning the lagoon and onto the coarse sand for spectacular views of the ocean and, in either direction, massive jutting rocks and the rugged windswept headlands.

On the hard wet sand at the waves' edge, we wandered to the southern end to view, close up, impressive Bird Rock and the natural cave carved through its base by centuries of relentlessly pounding surf. Against the cliffs is a great spot for a picnic.

Since the closure of the old one-way tunnel from Fort Baker to Fort Barry, one now has to take the spectacular road toward Point Bonita to reach Rodeo Beach. Turn off Hwy 101 just before the Golden Gate Bridge, or driving north, exit 101 and swing under it, to follow the GGNRA signs. You'll find it a rewarding journey.

Footsteps lead across the sand and end where two fishermen try their luck down by Bird Rock on a day of gentle surf.

MUIR BEACH

—————————————————————————————————— 4

small intimate look at the ocean

HERE IS AN unincorporated area of considerable charm, Marin at its seashore best.

Muir Beach, itself, is a quarter-mile arc of fine grey-brown sand tucked between high bluffs at either end, with a scattering of driftwood and logs. Actually there are two beaches, a big one with a little one to the north, separated by a series of jagged rocks that reach out into the breakers.

Use is regulated by the Golden Gate National Recreation Area. No camping, and a 10 p.m. closure. Swimming is dangerous because of rip currents. Ocean fishing is permitted, but none in the small fresh water lagoon in order to protect migrating steelhead and salmon.

You'll find a somewhat limited gravel parking area that ends facing the beach. There's a large grassy picnic meadow with tables and trash cans before you reach the sand by crossing a bridge that spans the creek.

The bluff to the south is nearly barren with a sign at the trailhead reading, "Area Closed to Restore Nature." Before the trail was closed, it led to Tennessee Valley Beach several miles to the south.

We were told by a native that both beaches are usually crowded weekends and that we might see some nudists at the little beach. Few were in evidence as it was a weekday.

We exited by way of a steep trail, and ended our walk admiring hillside homes and gardens, most with decks, some with retaining walls. Many diverging pathways led up and down the hillside in neighborly fashion somehow adding enchantment to the location.

Leaving the parking lot, we went past Pelican Inn, a fine English-style establishment with an authentic pub, seven charming rooms, a dining hall and glassed enclosed terrace for serving great meals. It's worth a stop.

Back on HWY 1, we continued north up the hill to Muir Beach Overlook.

To get to Muir Beach take twisting HWY 1 west out of Mill Valley for about five miles.

Looking down through the trees to the south end of Muir Beach where several people skirt the waves. Closed trail to Tennessee Beach is visible on the cliff.

MUIR BEACH OVERLOOK

5

on a clear day you can see forever

A STEEP CLIMB in your car takes you up HWY 1 to Seascape and the crest of the ridge above Muir Beach. You'll pass many-windowed homes of unusual designs, most befitting headlands ambiance. A small easy-to-miss sign on your left announces Muir Beach Overlook. Once you make the left swing, you're in for a surprise.

At first you won't see much except a paved parking loop with a large hilltop water supply tank, some portable privies and trash cans, one for recycled beverage containers. Clusters of pine and eucalyptus trees and coyote bush are in evidence. Just beyond, on the bare bluff, perch a few picnic tables. As you walk west, the powerful view comes into focus, a sweeping vista of Pacific Ocean from south to north. You're above it all but see the surf crashing against rugged rocks below and the Marin headlands stretching in either direction.

You'll come upon a World War II cement-domed lookout post, soon another and another. Then you're going down stairs fashioned from used railroad ties and a rail-guarded pathway leading to a pinnacle of rock and an unsurpassed panoramic view. A few small paths lead off to nearby knobby little peaks. The main trail ends in a fenced circle for you to rest and stand in awe of the magnificence spread below and far out to sea.

Back near one of the lookout structures, another protected trail leads east into a grove of cypress and Monterey pine. Each December here you'll see fluttering monarch butterflies en route to resting grounds far below in tall trees near Pelican Inn on the road to Muir Beach proper.

26

Suddenly you're in a secluded picnic area protected from the wind by gnarled old pines. A sturdy weathered table invites you to sit for a spell, to relax and hear the whisper of the wind through the treetops. You could even barbeque on the provided grill. What a grand spot for a picnic!

Below, through branches, you get a unique view of the small community of Muir Beach. Hillside homes are at your feet, clinging at various elevations above the beach.

An easy pathway leads the short distance back to the parking lot. You will have completed an unforgettable circle . . . and can once again look upon the face of Mount Tamalpais.

On the railed trail down to the viewing circle, part of the magnificent view — Point Bonita, the San Francisco hills, and on down the coast to Pacifica.

SLIDE RANCH

6

above the ocean, a teaching farm

NORTH OF MUIR BEACH, on a road off HWY 1, lie 134 diverse acres overlooking a spectacular stretch of rugged coastline. It was operated first as a dairy ranch, then belonged to the Nature Conservancy before coming under the jurisdiction of the Golden Gate National Recreation Area.

Now Slide Ranch is a complex dispensing environmental information, a unique hands-on approach to teaching children and adults how to link their personal daily lives to nature through food and clothing. Two types of programs are offered; on weekends, family farm days; weekdays, young groups, usually students, grades one through twelve. Basic programs run from one half to three days.

"Ecology, the science of the relationship between living organisms and their environments, is at the heart of the Slide Ranch curriculum," said Administrative Director Ross Herbertson.

What an ideal and scenic location for an educational facility of this nature. Here children learn how to fashion nutritious, delicious breads and rolls from dough they'll bake in outdoor ovens. They watch sheep being shorn, learn how to card and spin wool, enjoy a special friendly relationship with goats, sheep, chickens, ducks and turkeys, a touch of farm life as it was years ago. Yes, they'll even be asked to milk goats.

This entire complex is a unique mixture of corrals, barns, cypress groves, gardens, trails, chicken coops, quaint structures. In spring, fields of shoulder-high yellow mustard harbor red-winged blackbirds. The Pacific Ocean, with its fascinating tidepools, crashes along the rocky shoreline below. One trail leads south to a weathered geodesic dome, where on the edge of a cliff, three legless wooden seats invite you to rest.

You can walk to a beach from Slide Ranch and many students do, under guidance, to explore tidepools and learn of the sea's relationship to their environment.

A gravel road down from HWY 1 is narrow and steep but short. Parking, on a small flat area near a closed gate, is limited. No dogs allowed. All programs by reservation only. Call 381-6155.

Through a field of mustard beside the entrance road, we look down on a greenhouse, several residences and some of the tall trees, to the cliffs above the ocean, beaches and tidepools.

BOOTJACK

7

shady picnic spot with spectacular views

B OOTJACK, ON THE way to the top of Mount Tamalpais, is challenging, different — and far more spacious than first meets the eye. In fact, as an outdoor lover, you're in for a genuine surprise when you first visit.

In Mount Tamalpais State Park, this is an easy place to miss on winding Panoramic Road. A prominent outcropping of rock on the right is an indication you're almost there. Slow down and swing into a spacious paved parking area of about a 50-car capacity, a hint of what you can't see up the wooded hillside.

Signs indicate that this is a trailhead — .7 of a mile to Mt. Theater, 2.7 to Mt. Home, Stinson Beach 3.9, etc. There's a drinking fountain, convenient trash barrels, some fine rockwork including a sturdy stairway leading to five-star restrooms. They're clean and white with flush toilets, mirrors and paper towels.

The serpentine rock of the area, unearthed in making level spots for tables, has been artfully used in steps and path borders to enhance the flavor of the facility. Deceptively, it doesn't look as though there are many sturdy picnic tables spread beneath Douglas fir, oak, hazelnut and other trees with toyon and azalea in between. Yet follow any path and you'll soon see a table just right for the spot, be it a group picnic, or just plain seclusion in an sylvan setting.

30

There are little bridges, blacktop paths, a trickling stream, steep fenced trails, some finely terraced, leading up the hillside to even more tables. The group picnic area boasts an impressive stone barbecue complex with six grills! Tables are more closely grouped here.

The day my wife and I lunched there was special. Fog spread a blanket over the Pacific and Stinson Beach to the west. A pair of raucous stellar jays proclaimed territorial rights and demanded crusts from our sandwiches. The wine was smooth and tasty beneath the trees as we experienced a pronounced intimacy with nature.

As there was more of Marin to see up the road a piece, we pushed on, but the melody lingered . . .

Two hikers take the trail past tables in the group picnic area. Obscured by trees and the day's light fog is a view of hills, valleys and San Francisco's skyline.

PANTOLL RANGER STATION

8

park, hike, camp, relax

BESIDES BREATHTAKING views to the west, Panoramic Highway en route to the top of Mount Tamalpais offers many attractions to hikers, bikers, backpackers, picnickers, birders and campers.

Among the best is PanToll Ranger Station, Mount Tamalpais State Park. You'll find it where Panoramic splits a half mile beyond Bootjack Picnic Area, the high road continuing to the top of the mountain, the low road heading down to HWY 1 and Stinson Beach. The entrance to PanToll's expansive paved parking areas and walk-in uphill campsites is to your left. A flagpole marks the ranger station fronted by a shady, grassy fenced area. Nearby are trash cans, a drinking fountain and a clean cement building housing unisex restrooms.

There are 16 campsites, each equipped with sturdy tables, stone barbecue grills and food lockers. They are well-designed and all but hidden one from the other by heavy old growth forest. Paths are broad and shaded and gently lead to oak, fir and pine-studded knolls. Camps are on a first come first serve basis and are ideal for family camping, but on summer weekends are usually taken early. It's much less crowded and seemingly more secluded on spring, fall and winter weekdays.

Walk-in campsites are $12 per night, seniors 62 and over $10; en route camping, $10; Hike and Bike, Site #3, $3; dogs, $3; additional vehicle, $5; West Point parking, $5; day use parking, $5. There are also two group campsites, A and B.

If you need firewood, you can get it for $3 a bundle. The sign also warns of raccoons. Check out time is 2 p.m.

A short, easy walk will get you to any of the 16 campsites. Pre-registration is required so visit the ranger station first after parking your car. Courteous, cooperative rangers will answer your questions.

PanToll is a trailhead for several locations. Steep Ravine starts here. Trailheads are clearly marked with distances given in both kilometers and miles.

For more information, call 388-2070.

As secluded as it seems, one of the 16 campsites at PanToll. There is a wonderful feeling of being in the deep woods, far away from everything.

STEEP RAVINE

9

spirited creek, narrow canyon, towering trees

W E PAID THE $5 parking fee at PanToll Ranger Station and started out. "No dogs, bikes or horses," a sign read at Steep Ravine trailhead. Also, we saw we had 1.6 miles to Dipsea Trail, 2.0 to HWY 1.

We immediately entered a heavily wooded area, mostly Douglas fir and tall, skinny California laurel, with ferns everywhere. Soon the log-bordered trail plunged into the canyon by way of a series of well-maintained switchbacks.

From this point downward Jayne and I understood why no dogs, bikes or horses. It is truly a steep ravine! We encountered the first stately, veteran redwoods, sentinels standing straight and tall at the entrance to an intriguing adventure.

Our fascination grew as the magnificent descent unfolded to rugged forest splendor of significant proportions. Fallen bay trees arched over a trail that ducked and curved, crossing and recrossing Webb Creek over many bridges with protective wooden railings. Several structures were supported by long-running parallel steel "I" beams, the seventh such at Dipsea Trail junction.

Stone stairways, high ledges, tributary creeks and fascinating water-falls all contributed to the intriguing route. We even decended a ladder and then hunched over to squirm through a doorway hacked out of the trunk of a fallen giant redwood.

Just beyond the Dipsea Trail junction, a brackish pond appeared containing a pump housing. Here one trail veered away, leading toward Panoramic Highway high above. We took the narrow path closer to the creek, crossing two bridges. By now we had left the dense growth of redwoods, and were under oak and madrone, with willow and birch marking the creek. Wildflowers were more profuse — red columbine, forget-me-nots, miner's lettuce, and a covering of periwinkle, perhaps a garden escapee from artist Thaddeus Welsh's five years of living here in the early 1900's.

Suddenly the riparian growth gave way to grasses and coyote bush, and, beyond a hill, the ocean was in view. We reached HWY 1. After a brief rest we retraced our route, climbing slowly, savoring each step of the trip back.

One of the many waterfalls on Webb Creek. Ferns, little maples, huge rocks, delicate bushes, all under the towering redwoods and bays, make this a sylvan delight.

STEEP RAVINE
CAMPGROUND

—10

tidy cabins above the pounding sea

THE ENTRANCE ROAD is paved but narrow as its winds down the treeless headlands from HWY 1 toward the Pacific Ocean, ending on a bluff high above the crashing surf. You find yourself parked parked in a unique complex of ten rustic cabins and six campsites, a mile south of Stinson Beach.

The cabins have names like Dipsea, San Andreas, William Kent and Thaddeus Welch and are equipped with wood-burning stoves, table benches, wooden sleeping platforms and outdoor barbecues. Each campsite has a table and a barbecue stove.

You have arrived at Mount Tamalpais State Park Steep Ravine Environmental Campground. The cabins have no furniture, electricity or running water. Each is limited to five persons except for Cabin Three with a three-person maximum. Campsites are limited to five people. One car per cabin or camp. Primitive toilets and drinking water are nearby.

Distances are short from the parking area to the cabins and campsites. Stairs and a trail lead down to the beach. There are hazardous cliffs and the surf is dangerous. Watch out for poison oak. No dogs, trailers or RVs allowed. But you are surrounded by spectacular scenery and that wonderful feeling of belonging in the environmental sense. Living is primitive and adventurous here, salt-tinged air refreshing and invigorating. A pioneer spirit seems to prevail.

Those hiking down Steep Ravine Trail from PanToll Ranger Station, can cross HWY 1, and walk 50 yards to the sign. You'll find the entrance road gate locked since no vehicles are allowed except those with reservations. You can walk the road a piece and look down to where the cabins are nestled above the pounding surf. To drive and stay, however, reservations are required. You can register in person at the PanToll Ranger Station after 2 p.m. Or you can register and obtain the combination for the lock on the entrance gate by calling 456-5218 or toll free 1-800-444-7275 between 8 a.m. and 5 p.m. Monday through Friday. The cost is $25 per night for a cabin, $6 for an environmental campsite. Check-in time, 2 p.m., check-out noon.

From the entrance road looking down to the cluster of rustic cabins, perched on the cliff above the crashing sea. Stairs and path lead down to the sandy beach. Campsites are on the bluff to the left.

SAUSALITO PARKS

11

a string of spots to play along the bay

C AN A CITY with a hodgepodge of marinas, clubs, restaurants, boutiques and other businesses — all water-oriented, — still allow room for community parks along the precious waterfront?

Sausalito does. For lovers of wide-open spaces, the congestion may seem overwhelming. However, opportunity to walk, jog, sail, picnic, bike, sun, loaf and, in general, enjoy life, are all present here.

You can drive directly to parkways near Industrial Drive or you might want to start on the old Northwestern Pacific right-of-way, now a multi-use pathway, from Howard Johnson's beneath HWY 101 overpass at Richardson Bay, and head south on foot toward the old Marinship buildings and the Bay Model.

Recently my wife and I probed the area and were not disappointed. We found adequate paved parking, clean restrooms, and ample room for enjoyment.

Marinship Park has three active tennis courts with rules posted, a restroom and large grassy playing field behind a chainlink fence. Toward the bay, a wooden sign proclaims you're now in Shoreline Park with fine paved paths bordered with iceplants and low shrubs, berm-planted turf, weeping willows, poplar trees and cement-squared walkways.

I talked with the director of Sausalito Sailing Club. "We give rides and rent sailboats," he said. "How about coming along?"

Instead we opted to drive to Dunphy Park at the end of Napa Street. Here we found a play area, wide green lawns, a tiny beach, weeping willows, horseshoe pit, a brick barbecue and more, all honoring Earl F. Dunphy for his decades of dedicated public service.

Then it was back to the comparatively new Schoonmaker Point Marina beach, just beyond the Bay Model and behind the Schoonmaker complex, where a kayak regatta was in full swing. Here are 15 towering palms and an inviting sandy beach. A small two-story building, flags flying, houses a harbormaster upstairs with restrooms beneath.

We found each place a welcome respite, a spot to escape and feel unpressured, barely beyond the reach of the monotone sounds of heavy Bridgeway auto traffic.

The wide green lawn of Dunphy Park, looking under the spreading branches of a huge willow to the pilings protecting the tiny beach, and out to boats bobbing on the bay.

BOTHIN MARSH

————————————————————————— 12

a walk where water birds feed

INETY-THREE ACRE Bothin Marsh lies between Almonte, on the old Northwestern Pacific Railroad right-of-way and Howard Johnson's beneath the HWY 101 overpass at Richardson Bay.

To see it all, a good starting point is where the tracks once crossed Blithedale Avenue near Camino Alto in Mill Valley. Head south. It can be a rewarding outdoor experience to walk, jog, run, hike or bike for two miles on a wide, paved, nearly straight multi-use thoroughfare, part of Marin County Parks and Open Space.

No motor vehicles allowed but be aware that it is popular with bicyclists. In a short distance you'll come to Mill Valley's Bayfront Park, a splendid 19-acre recreation area at the end of Sycamore Avenue. A bit farther south is the beginning of Bothin Saltwater Marsh proper, a birder's paradise, particularly at low tide when a wide variety of feathered species do their thing.

Almonte is where the railroad branched off to Mill Valley. It was along here that *The Special* ran each school morning bringing students from Fairfax, San Anselmo, Ross and other central Marin County locations to Almonte and Tamalpais High School. My wife was an NWP commuter and recalls with a particular fondness, riding that electric train to classes in the late 1930's.

But now as you proceed southward there are sloughs on either side alive with crustaceans and birdlife. Chances are good you'll feel a cooling salt-tinged breeze fresh off of Richardson Bay. Almonte Highway parallels

40

your pathway some distance to the west. There's plenty of room to pause and take a few deep breaths and a sweeping 360 degree view from the middle of Bothin Marsh.

This is protected open space at its best, with great views in all directions, nature preserved for future generations.

Those sturdy bridges crossing sloughs enroute are protected with high wooden railings. On a flood tide, the walkway almost disappears and the adventurous hiker appears, from a distance, to walk upon the water.

As you near Howard Johnson's and HWY 101, you may want to continue on to Sausalito, or return as you came. Approached from the opposite direction, it has an entirely different aspect. Either way, you'll have an invigorating interesting outing.

A sturdy bridge as you start across Bothin Marsh. Here with HWY 101 at your back, Mount Tamalpais looms ahead. Around the point of dark trees is Almonte. To the right, just off the picture, is Bayshore Park.

BAYFRONT PARK

13

parcourse, rolling lawns & playing fields

B ISECTED BY THE northernmost tip of Richardson Bay, the nineteen beautifully planned acres of Bayfront Park, Mill Valley, are a perfect setting for joyful recreation.

One exciting aspect of the spread is a Parcourse Fitness circuit consisting of 18 stations. It's fun to read the instructions at each stop and, if you're dedicated, perform the exercise. Signs tell you the right number of tries for your condition. Don't overdo. There's even a heart rate check schedule at Station No. 1 for your guidance.

Then stroll across a beautiful arched bridge over the slough leading to the park's east side. Whether you're exploring the east or west side of the park, one of the 18 exercise stations is nearby. Along the waterfront you'll see clumps of pampas grass, cattails, patches of ice plant, sturdy benches facing the water, grassy knolls and cinder pathways winding through tawny fields.

I stopped at exercise station No. 5, the Log Hop, and found myself jumping over railroad ties. As a retired SP locomotive engineer, this seemed appropriate.

The Mill Valley Public Safety building and fire house form a nicely designed complex that faces west across the park. A bit farther north are clean, tiled restrooms built to also accomodate the handicapped, an outside drinking fountain and a paved parking area.

42

Hauke Park comprises about an acre of Bayfront's northeast corner where a great play area occupies a generous piece of manicured turf. There's a Little League ball diamond here and a superb place for tots to romp, with tubes, slides, swings and climbing structures. Nearby is a picnic table beneath a veteran eucalyptus tree.

The main entrance to Bayfront Park is at the end of Sycamore Avenue off of Camino Alto, just beyond the Mill Valley Middle School. No horses allowed but there is a dog-run area. Keep your animal on a leash.

Across a finger of the Bay, the pathway to Bothin Marsh and Sausalito runs behind the boat dock and out of the picture to the left. Playing fields are off to the right, as is the parcourse.

WALK TO ALTO TUNNEL

——————————————————— 14

where the trains once ran

AN UNUSUAL OUTDOOR experience, with a touch of history, is to walk, jog, run or bike the old Northwestern Pacific Railroad right-of-way north from Blithedale at Lomita in Mill Valley to the location of the old Alto tunnel, a distance of about a mile.

The beginning, comprising about half the journey, is Marin County Parks and Open Space multi-use pathway, wide and paved, on a slight ascending grade. Above on your left, out of sight, is Camino Alto twisting up and over the hill toward Corte Madera and Larkspur. To the right, suburban backyards give way to Mill Valley's Alto School, a broad stretch of playgrounds, and finally a tangle of blackberry bushes, willow and laurel.

Perhaps that doesn't sound too interesting, but to understand that you are treading on a rich stretch of Marin history should at least pique your curiosity.

This was NWP's double track electrified main line from Sausalito to San Anselmo and Manor or San Rafael, one of the most advanced ever for its time. Be on the lookout for an occasional square chunk of concrete upon which once stood a tall railroad light signal governing the movement of comfortable swift interurban trains.

There are many indications that this was a busy railroad, one we could certainly use now to help alleviate HWY 101 gridlock. But those signs, obliterated by time, are hard to recognize.

My wife and I walked the stretch recently and saw the cement slabs, all that's left of the boarding area at Alto station. We visualized where the tracks ran side by side, where the protective guard of the third rail was and estimated where rails converged to single track for the tunnel. We found a rotted old railroad tie, holes still evident where spikes secured rails to the roadbed.

The pavement now ends where a stop sign signals a new road, Vasco Court, which bisects the trail. From there on, the path is unpaved. Where the abandoned right-of-way swings gently left, willows, even cattails, have taken over. The ground becomes spongy, then downright wet, even during droughts. Suddenly you're against the hill, the tunnel's portal totally blocked by shale and dirt, like the ringing down of a cruel curtain on history.

We turned and retraced our steps somewhat sadly.

Where the path becomes damp, water sits in ruts and willows grow. Just beyond the bend, you come to the blocked tunnel.

BOYLE PARK

everything a place needs is here

MILL VALLEY can be proud of these 7.7 acres of well designed nicely maintained recreational facilities in a beautiful setting bisected by a creek. The entire complex is handicap accessible.

No bikes, motor vehicles or horses allowed and dogs must be leashed. There is room here for outdoor lovers to follow almost any pursuit. I was impressed by the five great public tennis courts. All were busy this bright weekday morning. Rules are clearly posted. Passes are required to play. Resident fees are $2 per day, $4 per month, $18 for six months, $33 per year; non-residents, slightly higher. This successful system was adopted in 1977. Fees help maintain the courts with resurfacing scheduled as needed.

The Debbie Play Area is dedicated to the happiness of the children of Mill Valley by the friends and family of Debbie Joseph who lived only from 1969 to 1972. It's a wonderful, safe place for tots. Nearby are baby swings and picnic tables beneath oak and bay trees. More tables adorn the north end of the turf area.

You can cross the creek on a wooden-railed bridge to a pair of well-groomed softball diamonds with bleachers and scoreboards.

This is the home of the Mill Valley Little League. There's an atmosphere of excitement here even when the diamonds and stands are empty, for you know they won't be that way long.

By the creek you'll see cement steps on either bank that once approached a bridge that no longer exists. A magnificent oak tree towers here just west of the turf. At the north perimeter of the complex you'll find an elaborate barbecue and group picnic area. In 1976 the local Lions Club built a large cement block and tiled facility. A barbecue pit stretches nearly 30 feet with two sinks, five double electrical outlets and a tiled L-shaped serving area.

In 1991, additional parking and fencing was added at the Little League complex. For this side of the park, enter off Blithedale at Thalia and make a right turn. Construction of additional parking, a new pro-shop and restrooms on the east side by the tennis courts also took place in 1991. There's a one way entrance to the park off Blithedale on East Drive. Or, opposite Park School on Blithedale, take Elm Avenue and turn left on East Drive into the parking area. Phone 383-1370 for more information.

Near the creek, one corner of expansive and varied Boyle Park. Barbecue facilities are off to the right, playground behind, and Little League diamonds, over the bridge to the left.

OLD MILL PARK

history under the redwoods

ANOTHER DISTINCTIVE PARK worth visiting encompasses 7.4 acres beneath splendid groves of second growth redwoods, with a sandy playground area offering swings, slides, interesting climbing structures, and picnic tables plus other attractions.

Old Mill Park is rich in history. Located at Throckmorton Avenue and Cascade Drive, it contains the site of John Reed's more than 150-year-old mill, recently restored. You'll be fascinated by the huge timbers that support the mill's steep roof. Remains of an old cement dam abutment no longer retard the gurgling waters of Cascade Creek that flow the length of the park. A Tamalpais & Muir Woods gravity car from the long-defunct "crookedest railroad in the world," is on permanent display nearby.

This is a great place to relax beneath the tall stately redwoods that keep the park shaded nearly all the time.

Adjacent to the playground area, new pre-fab custom-designed restrooms were recently constructed.

Near the playground, mounted on a large stone, is a plaque reading, "In memory of Clarc Ropers — 1971-1980." There is something special about a memorial to a child where children play.

A walk northward brings you to an ampitheater. The stage faces rows of logs for audience seating.

Old Mill is the location of Mill Valley's Fall Art Festival, a popular annual event held each September. The two-day fair features all sorts of artistic endeavors.

You'll find an outstanding library on Throckmorton Avenue overlooking the park that definitely deserves a visit. Designed by architect Donn Emmons, the impressive structure was completed in 1966. High windows, great views from within, and sculptures of black and grey granite near the entrance, designed by Richard O'Hanlon, grace the building.

If you're a history buff, be sure to visit this public library. The Mill Valley Historical Society is active in collecting old photos, books and other memorabilia.

Old Mill Park is open from sunrise to sunset. For more information call 383-1370.

Shaded by tall redwoods, above the flowing waters of Cascade Creek, stands John Reed's old mill. This is just one of many attractions at Old Mill Park.

CASCADE FALLS

enchanted walk in the misty woods

ON A COLD FEBRUARY afternoon with intermittent rain, not the kind of day you would ordinarily be seeking an exciting outdoor experience, we found one anyway.

My wife and I had heard about Cascade Falls, and as we were driving through Mill Valley, decided to search out Cascade Park.

We swung left off Throckmorton Avenue onto Cascade Drive and crossed a creek on the bridge just above John Reed's historic millsite marked by a sturdy old structure beside the stream.

Once over the bridge, Cascade Drive swings right and from there on the road is curvy and narrow, no sidewalks here, with multi-storied, elegant homes clinging to either side of the canyon. Drive carefully for even this cold weekday afternoon found pedestrians, mid-street, enjoying beauty beneath straight tall trees with their damp, delicately-scented leaves and needles.

Slightly less than a mile from Old Mill Park, and just a tenth of a mile from where Throckmorton ends on Cascade, you'll see a wide space on your right, room enough to park three or four cars. This is it although nothing remains of the Cascade Falls sign except the post it was attached to.

Ours was the lone vehicle. We parked and started on foot up the spongy path, the nearby creek chuckling happily down the rocky course.

A short walk through the forest, rather steep in places, with ferns

50

carpeting the hillsides, brought us to where the trail splits.

Jayne took the high path to the left. I, the low on the right, soon crossing a sturdy wooden footbridge to stand, gazing in delight at the waterfall, lively from the rain, a frisky wide ribbon of water plunging straight to the tumbling creek below.

Jayne crossed the footbridge above the falls and circled down to stand silently beside me. For a few magic moments we drank in all the splendor of nature, a symphony of sights, scents and sounds, hushed and misty.

Then we parted to complete the two-bridge loop from opposite directions, meeting back where the trail split, joyfully ending an unexpected and invigorating outdoor adventure . . .

*Cascade Falls,
plunging 30 feet to
the pool below, is
an exciting sight.
A bridge on the
upper path crosses
above the falls and
circles down to the
creek below.
A favorite spot for
artists.*

BLACKIE'S PASTURE

18

memorial to a well-loved horse

W HO WAS BLACKIE and how did his pasture become so famous?

I stopped to find out recently and was surprised at the huge gravelled parking area with paved bike paths heading east. It's at Tiburon Boulevard and Trestle Glen named after a high trestle that once served busy Northwestern Pacific Railroad traffic.

It was a day following a heavy storm and there were large puddles everywhere. Muddy water swirled toward Richardson Bay beneath the bridge spanning a slough. Boat wreckage from recent high winds was strewn along the shoreline.

Here begins the Parcourse Fitness Area with 18 stations stretching and circling for a couple of miles. But what about Blackie?

I saw the white picket fence to the north of me surrounding a small plot of ground. Dodging puddles, I was soon standing before a large rock centered by a bronze plaque picturing a sway-back horse. "Blackie," the words beneath read, "1933 — died Feb. 1966. A perpetual memorial to a horse beloved by children and adults alike."

Blackie is buried here, acknowledged by a big plain sign bearing his name. Someone had recently put flowers at the gravesite. The fence surrounding the small plot was gleaming white and wet with rain. I felt a sudden reverance I wasn't expecting. My eyes travelled from the plaque to the plot and back several times.

Finally I left Blackie and walked a mile along the old NWP right-of-way to meet my wife. Somehow I found myself wondering how the horse and the train crews got along. I'll bet he responded to a steam whistle and the engineer's friendly wave in a special way.

At the car, Jayne said, "I brought all five of my children here to see Blackie when they were little. Cathi still remembers the heaps of flowers on his grave when we came down after his death. They loved that horse, and so did everyone else in Marin back then."

The huge rock and bronze plaque in front of the picket fence that marks Blackie's grave. The beloved horse was much more sway-backed than shown on the plaque.

LINEAL PARK

popular path parallels the bay

HARD TO TELL where Blackie's Pasture ends and the 55-acre Richardson Bay Lineal Park begins. But one thing is certain, it's two measured and marvelous miles from the large gravelled parking area just off Tiburon Boulevard at Trestle Glen to Tiburon, mostly along the scenic old Northwestern Pacific Railroad right-of-way.

Start at the Parcourse Fitness Area, cross the slough on a wooden bridge and head east. You'll see a wildlife enhancement project on your left. The broad paved path is great for hiking, jogging, biking and sightseeing. If you stay to the right taking the gravelled path you'll cling to the shore of Richardson Bay where a variety of seabirds are always in evidence.

The shoreline is protected from erosion with large rocks and a sign tells you the prominent grassy field is kept green with reclaimed water. Convenient benches face the bay from many locations.

I stopped at Parcourse Fitness Station No. 5 and did the "Loghop" as instructed. It was like jumping over railroad ties, and I've always liked that. Then I sat on a nearby bench and in complete solitude scanned the bay from Strawberry Point in the distance to Sausalito and Belvedere Island. What a glorious sweep, Marin at its finest.

Beyond, around a bay-hugging bluff, I came to Station No. 7, "Circle Body." Didn't try this one because I was fascinated by the play area constructed at the base of the hill — swings, rings, slides and other sturdy structures for kids. Nearby is McKegney Green. Permits are required for organized sports here.

Now all paths merge into a broad, paved level one exactly on the old NWP right-of-way. Tiburon Boulevard and the walkway are separated by homes along here. Then you come to a whole block of tennis courts on your left. Off to the other side is the bay, the Sausalito shoreline backed by hills and San Francisco's skyline.

This crisp winter morning a few dog-walkers were being yanked along by frisky leashed animals.

I stopped at a bench facing the bay for a moment. There was a bronze plaque in cement beside it that read simply "Maidella."

Pretty name, I thought. Wonder who she was?

Tiburon end of Richardson Bay Lineal Park, with towering clouds over Mount Tamalpais. This is a popular early morning walkway and an invigorating place any time.

ELEPHANT ROCK

ring around the rock, a platform for kids

W HERE IS ELEPHANT Rock? What is it? Many Marin sports-
people know, particularly those with children who like to fish.
But others, even if they've seen it in passing, may not.

Well, it's an innovative structure fashioned around a rock, somewhat
resembling an elephant, a few yards offshore in Raccoon Strait at the tip
of the hilly Tiburon Peninsula opposite Angel Island. Dedicated to the
memory of Robert (Bunkie) Keener, it is reserved for young anglers
under 16. Others may fish there but the priority belongs to youth, and
we're for that.

This is an intriguing spot for all ages because the rocky shore west of
the pier extends clear to the Tiburon ferry landing and is popular with
shore anglers.

I first saw this ingenious architectual accomplishment a few years
ago on a winter day following one of the last big herring runs in years, in
the company of Bill Groth and two other veteran Ross anglers.

Remnants of herring roe still clung to the rocks and we were hoping
to legally scoop up some of the writhing creatures for the table and for
future bait uses.

Bill Groth was tossing a Hawaiian circular net with some precision
but still coming up empty handed. The rest of us, baited with herring,
were trying for sturgeon without success.

An hour of close fellowship, the kind anglers share the world over,
followed. But most important was the fact we were near home. And at

our feet was the possibility of catching rockfish, striped bass, sturgeon or other species.

Tides on the move run swiftly here, and there's always plenty to hold your attention — historic Tiburon and Belvedere, Angel Island, seabirds circling, diving, squawking, the magnificance of outdoors in one of its finest moods.

Stop and walk the circular pier at Elephant Rock. It'll do you good. Talk to any young anglers and see how they feel. Smell the salt-tinged air. Let your eyes wander east, west and every way. Absorb the atmsophere, the beauty, the wonder.

The only losers are those trapped in the HWY 101 snarl. Elephant Rock is a worthwhile detour. Check it out.

The railed platform around Elephant Rock. A tip of Angel Island across Raccoon Straits, is visible and, in the distance, the skyline of San Francisco.

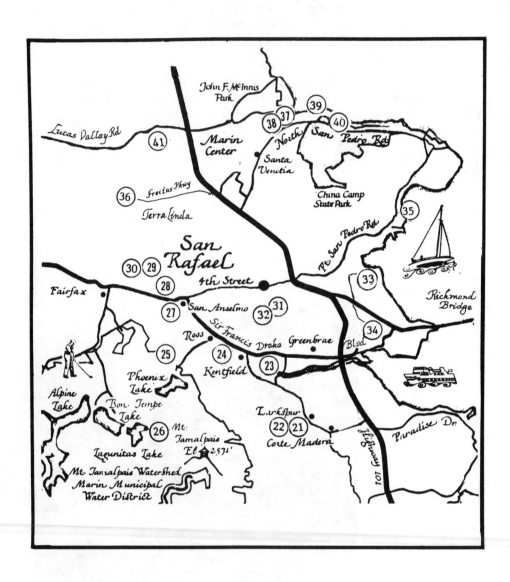

John F. McInnis Park

Lucas Valley Rd

38 37 39 40

41

Marin Center

North

San Pedro Rd

Santa Venetia

China Camp State Park

36 Freitas Pkwy

Terra Linda

35

San Rafael

Pt San Pedro Rd

30 29

28

Fairfax

4th Street

Richmond Bridge

27 San Anselmo

33

32 31

Ross

Sir Francis Drake

Greenbrae

Blvd

34

25

24

Kentfield

23

Phoenix Lake

Alpine Lake

Bon Tempe Lake

26

Mt. Tamalpais
El. 2571'

Larkspur

22 21

Corte Madera

Paradise Dr.

Lagunitas Lake

Mt. Tamalpais Watershed
Marin Municipal
Water District

Highway 101

58

CENTRAL MARIN

DOLLIVER PARK

deep in the woods, close to town

ONE OF MARIN's best kept secrets is an enchanting 2-1/2 acres beneath towering redwoods and Caifornia laurels in downtown Larkspur. Called Dolliver Park, unless you look closely, you'll miss the spot. Where Madrone Avenue branches west off Magnolia, it bisects the park. Tall redwoods are actually paved around and stand in the roadway!

What's here beside trees, outdoors folks may wonder? There's seclusion, shade, comfort, picnic tables, restrooms, a drinking fountain, and a safe, elaborate playground for your kids with a spiral slide, sandboxes, swings and other approved recreational structures.

Larkspur Creek, which meanders through, is either lazy or dry right now, but adds flavor to the setting either way. Just across Magnolia Avenue is famed Lark Creek Inn with all its Victorian splendor.

The most intriguing aspect of mini-Dolliver is its proximity to downtown Larkspur — just a few steps and you're into all the town has to offer, and that's a lot — bookstores, travel agencies, exotic places for lunch or dinner, just a nice easy going complex that can easily fulfill almost any need.

I strolled from Dolliver Park to City Hall and asked a few questions. "Kids call it 'Dark Park,'" said affable Nancy Spivey of Parks and Recreation. "They love the place."

Ellen Dolliver Jewell deeded the north portion to the city in 1923 providing there would be no buildings, and that trees be preserved, grounds maintained for recreational use only. The area south of Madrone was given by C.S. Burtchael, grandson of Thomas Dolliver, in 1956.

Ellen Jewell labelled her donation to Larkspur, "The first redwood grove on the Redwood Highway."

Then it was. Now HWY 101 runs a mile or so east, which largely accounts for the compact seclusion of this little gem. It's a superb spot for some outdoor R & R, especially when the weather is sizzling elsewhere.

Part of the playground can be seen behind the tall trunks of redwoods. This is a wonderful place to relax or picnic on a hot summer day when you haven't time for a big get-away.

DAWN FALLS TRAIL

22

stroll beneath redwoods to a rich reward

F ROM EITHER DIRECTION off Magnolia, swing onto Madrone Avenue opposite Lark Creek Inn and drive to the turnaround at the road's end, a bit less than one mile. There's a wide spot for a few cars. Park and start walking west. You're in for something special.

Cross the footbridge and head up along the old logging road on the left bank of Larkspur Creek, a spirited gusher following heavy rains, a lazy whispering stream in drier seasons, sometimes disappearing entirely on stretches. Pass through the wide opening in the fence with a sign granting access from sunrise to sunset.

Not far beyond, where the road dwindles into an easy trail beneath veteran redwoods, watch on the stream side for an unusual natural phenomenen — three trees entangled almost into one, two of them still alive and growing, and all wearing different hats.

Close inspection indicates the maple on the right side of the trail probably fell first, then a madrone from the opposite direction, followed by a California laurel (bay) rooted left of the trail. This last tree forms a long graceful arc over the path, then dips for an eventual twisting embrace with the maple and the madrone, the latter the only deceased tree of the trio.

This unusual quirk of nature drew our attention both going and coming on the 45-minute mile-and-a-half hike to Dawn Falls, another of Marin's hidden treasures. But shortly before our goal, in a spacious creekside redwood grove, next to a great slab of gray rock, were many pre-cut limbs to use as walking sticks for the steep climb up switchbacks to our ultimate reward.

We took our hike two weeks after the record-breaking March 1991 storms but because of five previous years of drought, the twenty-plus inches of rain had already been slurped up by an ultra-dry forest floor.

Nonetheless, my wife, Jayne, and I were thrilled by the beauty of Dawn Falls — a fine noisy ribbon of water dropping vertically and unobstructed for twenty feet or so with many mini-falls of far lesser magnitude stepping down from above.

We returned to the spot a month later and found just a trickle of water so be sure to take your hike on a sunny day at the height of a wet season. We have yet to get a picture of the falls.

Dawn Falls Trail beside an almost dry Larkspur Creek. We were delighted with the beauty of the walk, but saddened by the lack of water in the falls. Next time?

CREEKSIDE PARK

23

small park with a mountain view

ANOTHER OF MARIN's elusive outdoor spots is Creekside Park. Perhaps you drive by it almost daily without knowing it's there. How easy to miss the sturdy attractive carved wooden sign at the entrance, surrounded by rocks and landscaping, where a path for biking, jogging or hiking leads off through 26 gentle acres.

You miss it because Bon Air Road is busy in both directions between Sir Francis Drake Boulevard and Corte Madera Creek. And that's where Creekside Park is — on the Kentfield side, north of the road.

Ross Valley Swim and Tennis Club borders the park to the east, marshland farther north, Bon Air Road and Marin General Hospital on the south. Within these borders there is spaciousness to enjoy many kinds of outdoor recreation — broad expanses of rolling lawns, a small complex of three sturdy picnic tables, and a wonderful playground, just west of the tennis courts.

Paved and gravelled paths, some rock-bordered, wind between knolls with great views of Mount Tamalpais to the west from nearly any point in the park. You'll enjoy a variety of trees and plants and see some impressive landscaping.

A great spot to rest and reflect on the surrounding beauty is the overlook with its bench and terraced hillside. A sturdy railing is provided for support as you study a salt marsh below with Corte Madera Creek beyond.

Information covering wildlife, plants and animals is posted on both sides of four billboards housed beneath a common conical shingled roof. A master plan of the park is also posted, along with maps of Marin's bike paths, depicting the three types: Class I-bike paths, Class II-bike lanes, and Class III-shared routes. The maps also contain safety tips and other information.

Should the 26 acres not satisfy your exercise needs, the Bon Air VitaCourse parallels Corte Madera Creek just a short distance to the west. With many stations, it stretches a measured mile between College Avenue in Kentfield and Bon Air Road.

A portion of the picnic area, taken in February while the young trees are leafless. The playground is off to your left.

ROSS TO COLLEGE OF MARIN WALK

24

bike path along a channeled creek

A FINE OUTDOOR jaunt any time is between Ross post office and College of Marin along Corte Madera Creek.

If you haven't done it, try. If you have, undoubtedly you'll do it again and again for a lot of reasons.

A good one is the historic scenario. This was driven home to me in 1989 at the 100th anniversary of postal service in Ross. A noteworthy celebration, with the vintage fire engine on hand and a calliope breathing appropriate old songs under the talented fingers of Peter Clute. Postmaster Judith Goldstein and her helpers were acknowledged and honored. As there is no home delivery, Ross Post Office has a unique position in the social life of the town.

Speeches were given that day by the Ross Historical Society historian Carla Ehat who underscored the importance of early day railroading.

No wonder I came away all fired up to walk down the old North Pacific Coast railroad's narrow gauge right-of-way, which later was broadgauged for Northwestern Pacific electrics, commuter trains to San Francisco and return, that could beat, hands down time-wise, today's HWY 101 gridlock each morning and evening. I wish we still had them — those comfortable, swift, stress-free electrics!

Regardless, the multi-use paved pathway along Corte Madera Creek is exactly on the old railroad easement, enters Frederick S. Allen Park which ends at the tennis courts. En route on your right you'll enjoy the strip that contains acacias, pines, poplars, oaks, toyon berry bushes, buckeye and other growth.

You then pass behind Kentfield Medical hospital and parking area. A sign cautions to walk bikes here and beyond the wheelchair ramp that gently dips to continue south toward College of Marin.

All this time Corte Madera Creek is harnessed between cement walls on your left, part of an earlier flood control project that does not extend north beyond the southern extremity of the Ross parking lot.

This I know: The roundtrip is a bit more than a mile, a walk that outdoor lovers shouldn't miss. I didn't and I'm glad.

The curved pathway just as it starts in Ross, heading south along Corte Madera Creek, on the left, toward College of Marin in Kentfield. This is an easy pleasant walk.

BALDY

steep climb to a gentle summit

KNOW WHERE BALDY is? A grassy hump, seen to the right of Mount Tamalpais' silhouette from many points in central Marin, it has particular meaning for me.

I first saw its bare crest from my grandparents' home at 24 Austin Avenue, San Anselmo, the summer of 1923. I'd just turned six. Baldy's summit back then seemed miles high, with cattle grazing at the top.

Now I live with my wife, Jayne, just two blocks from the old homestead. Seldom a day passes that I don't look up at Baldy and nod thanks in a special way. My youthful fascination has mellowed into fond appreciation.

Sometimes called Mount Bald or Bald Hill, Baldy is a sentinel, overlooking much of Marin. Hike there and you'll see. You're not likely to find company should you decide to take the trek. Better bring a lunch and binoculars to enjoy a picnic and the view while you rest at the top. The grass will be either green or dry, depending upon the season. A clear, crisp winter day is a good time. The crystal air and the impressive panorama will make you reluctant to leave.

If you love exercise, natural beauty and a leisurely afternoon, park your car near the tennis courts at the end of Lagunitas Avenue, Ross. Walk west to Natalie Greene Park, up the road on the right to the dam at Phoenix Lake. Bear right on Worn Spring Road, climb, then go left through a gate and proceed upward.

Stay right to the top of Baldy. Settle down for some contemplation, picking out landmarks in the magnificence that spreads below you.

When ready to leave, backtrack to the first junction and bear right in an easterly direction. Soon you'll be in oaks and eventually come to a gate, pavement and a sudden transition to civilization. You're on Oak Avenue now which goes down to Austin Avenue. There you make a right for a block down the hill to Upper Road. Right again, up hill and down until you meet Glenwood. Right again, over the newly re-illuminated bridge, to Lagunitas and your car, having covered about four miles. In so doing you'll have seen some of the best views central Marin has to offer.

A view of Baldy from near our home in Ross. You can see the trees creeping up to the crown, providing cover that will, in time, contradict the gentle mountain's name.

PILOT KNOB TRAIL

26

top of the hill, top of the world

F OR AN EXTRAORDINARY outdoor experience, hike Pilot Knob trail above Lake Lagunitas. In that short distance you'll scarcely believe the changing scenes nature provides. On the high plateau, you'll seem to be eye-level with Mount Tamalpais across the canyons.

Park in the paved area below the dam adjacent to the redwood grove and picnic grounds. Stay left en route to the dam, and once there, climb the rock stairs below the ranger's residence and onto Lakeview Road which skirts Lagunitas with many impressive views.

It's pleasant level walking now beneath aged madrone, bay and oak trees as the road winds around coves and breaks out in the open near the head of the 23-acre lake. Stay left where the road forks to encircle Lagunitas.

The trail to Pilot Knob is on your left and clearly marked. You'll climb steeply through the woods with a wide variety of plants, trees and pleasing odors. At the crest of the knoll, an unmarked trail to the left leads you to Pilot Knob proper, elevation 1217 feet. Take it. The short, steep climb bursts into a seldom matched panorama which includes Lake Lagunitas, straight down, Mount Tamalpais, heavily wooded watershed lands and a great sweep of Marin County and the East Bay far below.

When ready, retrace your steps to the junction and bear left for a bigger surprise, a magnificent madrone that we wrote about in *Point Bonita to Point Reyes*. The six incredibly large, twisted trunks stemming from a massive base will more than likely keep you entranced.

The return trip is an easy, pleasing hike, mostly downhill, back to the parking lot. Bear right where the trail meets the road. Watch your footing, the road is slippery here from leaves and needles and quite steep. You'll have to brace your knees to put the brakes on.

The parking lot with your car is just below. Relax here for a moment. This is a good place to reflect the wonders of your 2.2 mile "enchanted circle" hike.

The author sits on a boulder, making notes on the climb to Pilot Knob. It's a steep drop down to Lagunitas Lake in the canyon, then up to Mount Tamalpais on the other side. Beyond views of Marin to the left, is a spectacular spread reaching across the shining waters to the east bay hills.

ROBSON HARRINGTON PARK

27

old-fashioned stateliness, new-fangled gardening

N EAR THE CORNER of Crescent Road and Raymond Street in San Anselmo, behind a splendid old stone wall, stands the magnificent, historic 17-room Robson-Harrington home built in 1910 by Edwin Wood. The Kernan Robsons bought the place in 1922, terracing the hillside with distinctive garden plots.

There's much to see in the 2-1/2 acres that belong to Robson Harrington City Park. Gracing the place you'll find glazed brickwork, arches, walls, hedges, brick-bordered pathways, mosaic plaques, tile fountains, even one with a spectacular sundial. There are spacious lawns, palms, redwoods and a variety of other trees, community-member maintained vegetable and flower gardens, picnic tables, a large playground and, at the lower corner of the lot, a brick-enclosed barbecue area.

There is also a list of restrictions — no motorized vehicles, no commercial use, no amplified sound, no volleyball, no horses, no alcohol, dogs on leash only, etc.

For outdoor lovers then, is it worth visiting?

Indeed it is. Those very restrictions add to your enjoyment if you're seeking a relaxing experience in peaceful, impressive surroundings.

Currently the mansion is governed by the Robson-Harrington House Association, Inc., the upstairs portion occupied by select service-oriented groups. Other areas of the home are rented for meetings but not weddings.

You'll find entrances to the park on Crescent Road facing the mansion, one on Raymond and several at the bottom of the hill off Tamalpais Avenue adjacent to the large green playing field.

On the hilltop east of the mansion is a paved, fenced overlook with benches offering a great view of the park below and beyond. A sandy children's playground with swings, structures of chained-together tires and a barrel slide, is available for play. Elaborate flower gardens are nearby.

The park is open from a half hour before sunrise to a half hour after sunset. Permission is needed for groups of 25 or more and a fee is required. For more information call 453-9055.

The trunk of a huge palm beside one of the many benches which add to the comfort of this small park. Looking across a piece of the lawn, a corner of the old mansion is visible.

SAN ANSELMO MEMORIAL PARK

28

a complete complex for play & relaxation

T HERE'S A NINE-acre expanse of well-groomed grass beckoning outdoor lovers, a time-proven spread in San Anselmo, the city's Memorial Park.

Walking it all on a recent Saturday morning, I found something special about the place. Perhaps it was the fact that almost every type of recreation is covered in some way or another — tennis courts, a basketball court, picnic tables, horseshoe pits, a fenced sandy playground for kids with swings and other sturdy, safe fun structures to develop young muscles while encouraging and challenging body-building.

There are clean restrooms and three baseball diamonds, good bleachers and scoreboards. The broad green fields sometimes double, I am told, for soccer, football and other games.

I had a brief exchange with a gentleman who has lived adjacent to the complex since 1951. He looks upon the entire nine acres with fond appreciation, mostly, it seems, because it has furnished him breathing and relaxing space through the years.

Going west on Sir Francis Drake Boulevard just beyond Redhill Shopping Center swing right at the stoplight on San Francisco Boulevard, go two blocks, turn right and you're in a fine paved parking area. Isabel Cook Community Center faces Sir Francis Drake and houses, among other things, San Anselmo's Parks and Recreation Department and the town's active Chamber of Commerce.

This impressive city park is bordered on the east by veteran eucalyptus, cypress and redwood trees. A prime point of interest at this memorial park is American Legion Post 179's rustic Boy Scout log cabin, dedicated May 27, 1934, and the adjacent World War II artillary pieces dedicated to the memory of Mary R. Torrance. For years, Thanksgving dinners have been served here to all who come.

The cabin, with its well-chinked logs, also harbors a dugout below. "Open every Monday and Friday at 6 p.m." a sign says.

I wonder what mysteries linger here?

American Legion log cabin at the back corner of San Anselmo Memorial Park with the WW II artillery pieces displayed in front. This is a popular spot for receptions and parties. In the summer of 1941, I folk danced here every Wednesday evening, even drank wine in the "dugout" below.

SORICH RANCH PARK

lone tree atop enormous rock

S ORICH RANCH PARK in San Anselmo is special — 63 acres of open space offering much within its perimeter. Just beyond Red Hill Shopping Center, turn right on San Francisco Boulevard and drive to the very end. Here the road encircles a towering jagged rock outcropping, a small tree standing guard at the summit.

There's parking room for a number of cars. To the left, surrounded by young redwoods and Portugese laurel, is the secluded grassy picnic area. It's a small flat at the foot of a mini-canyon with a brook that gurgles following winter and spring storms. A sign with a map and log fence posts mark the park entrance.

Beyond, oak-studded rounded hills rise steeply with trails leading off in various directions. Clearings are green in spring with a variety of wildflowers adding impressive touches of color here and there. By summer, grass turns tawny and will remain so until the first rains once again set the stage for the rebirth of green.

A broad, level gravelled area in a canyon at the base of the hills to the right of the parking space is closed to traffic. Adjacent is where you'll see the beginning results of a tree planting program, part of a continuous effort to improve the park by the San Anselmo Open Space and Marin Releaf committees. Silk, valley and white oaks and buckeye have been planted along with other trees and shrubs.

According to San Anselmo Open Space Committee's newsletter, Sorich is finally getting the attention it deserves following years of neglect and misuse. This committee is working with the Department of

Parks and Recreation to fashion the lower portions of the area for picnicking and passive recreation.

The continuous effort to improve the park by volunteers and various groups is evident. It grows better and more inviting with each passing season, a nearby place which offers seclusion and escape without the need of travelling miles.

For the hardy, the steep trails offer fine views from above and are worth the climb. Up here the beauty of Marin spreads below you in a special, memorable manner . . .

Secluded and grassy, the small picnic area left of the entrance to Sorich Ranch Park. A little creek runs in the gully behind the redwood tree when conditions are right. Sorich stretches to the top of the steep hills with many great trails.

FAUDE PARK

30

ridges, knolls & spectacular views

S AN ANSELMO HAS done well preserving open space for relaxation. Within the four city parks, ranging in size from just a few acres to many, you're bound to find something immensely to your liking.

My wife, Jayne, and I are intrigued by C. Frederick Faude Park, twenty rolling, wooded acres we find extremely worth visiting, steep as some of the trails are. As it was a weekday following a refreshing storm when we last visited, there wasn't another soul around to share the nippy air and magnificent view of the towns below and the wooded hills beyond, where splashes of fresh green grass triumphantly sprouted.

We lacked a blanket or ground cover to spread at any of the prime spots for a picnic, or simply to view a panorama of impressive magnitude. So we ambled slowly, taking pictures framed by the twisted branches of veteran oaks. There was Drake High School below us, Sir Francis Drake Boulevard stretching to Fairfax and beyond. With a slight twist of the head we could clearly see Red Hill, both San Anselmo Memorial and Sorich Ranch Parks with county open space beyond.

Our gaze, however, kept returning to Mount Tamalpais, directly across Ross Valley, magnificently flaunting puffy clouds piled on her crest.

All too soon our stimulating interlude ended. But not without a feeling of gratitude to C. Frederick Faude for donating this picturesque and secluded parcel to San Anselmo.

To visit Faude Park, drive west on Sir Francis Drake Boulevard to one stop light beyond Drake High School. Turn right on Broadmoor Avenue, go several blocks to Indian Rock Drive, right again and up the hill to Tomahawk Drive. Note blue sign on high pole that reads: "Faude Park Open Space Preserve." The arrow points right.

The entrance is where Alice and Elk Horn Ways meet. Limited parking. Foot traffic only from here. Chain blocks old road.

This is the same spot as shown in the cover photo and typical of the beautiful views seen from the ridge at Faude Park. The ancient oak was on the verge of leafing and wild flowers were sprouting at our feet.

ALBERT PARK

31

organized sports or total relaxation

D OWNTOWN SAN RAFAEL probably has one of the best compact recreational facilities anywhere for sport and outdoor lovers.

It lies between B Street and Lindaro and can be reached by heading east off B Street on one-way Albert Park Lane. You'll find many parking spaces to your left.

Care to play softball? Tennis? Jog? Run? Stroll? Feed ducks and pigeons? See wildlife? Let your kids play on slides, swings and other safety oriented structures? Picnic? Barbecue? Or plain laze it up in the open?

You can do them all here in a nicely designed complex that certainly gives you better than average alternatives.

I'm talking about Albert Park and all that it encompasses.

This 11.5-acre facility was donated to San Rafael in 1937 by Jacob Albert and the city chose to make good use of it. Now we have something worthwhile to enjoy any day of the week any time of the year from sunrise to sunset.

There are four tennis courts under the jurisdiction of the San Rafael Recreation Department. Group lessons are conducted on Courts 1 & 2 only. Rules are posted on Lindaro Street court entrances. Call 405-3333 for additional information.

The baseball diamond is impressive with its bleachers and tall lights. Many exciting games are held here. Use of the fields are by permit only.

West of the field proper lies a kid's paradise — sandy play areas with swings, a spiral slide and all kinds of room to romp and play. There's a large paved oval for walking and jogging, a pagoda covering a line of picnic tables. Terraced lawns with a variety of eye-pleasing trees and shrubs are well-kept and in evidence everywhere. Dogs must be leashed.

Across Albert Park Lane and a separating waterway to the south is the Marin Wildlife Center, a fascinating sanctuary where sick or injured birds and animals are restored to health and then released to their natural habitat.

Indeed there's much to see and enjoy here, all of it underscored for your outdoor enjoyment.

A small part of the huge complex with Albert Park Lane to the right. A piece of a playground area, a bench-box for sitting under one of the many trees, and the tall poles for night-lights on the ballfield are shown in this small glimpse of the 11-acre spread.

GERSTLE MEMORIAL PARK

32

botanical garden, playgrounds & redwoods

A SPACIOUS, LOVELY garden spot within the heart of San Rafael with well-designed facilities made for your enjoyment, Gerstle Memorial Park is an ideal place for outdoor recreation and the only botanical garden open to the public in Marin.

Traveling south on D Street, turn right on San Rafael Avenue and drive two blocks to Clark. The park is on your left, fronted by a fine rock wall and pipe railing. A stone stairway marks the main entrance.

Paved, brick-bordered paths wind among spacious lawns and flower beds and beneath a variety of large, beautiful trees, many shading picnic tables.

The six-acre parcel was once the grounds for a summer home owned by the Gerstle family. Hannah Gerstle lived there until her death in 1930, after which heirs gave the property to the city. History is preserved here in the form of a large-windowed building at the east end that houses a pair of early horse-drawn San Rafael fire engines.

In a cathederal of tall, straight redwoods, nine long picnic tables in two rows with barbecue facilities are comfortably situated and can be reserved for group picnics by calling 485-3333. Nearby are more tables beneath a wisteria covered arbor with a herringbone patterned brick floor.

On a hillside at the south border is a single tennis court reserved for San Rafael residents. Decals are issued to stick on tennis rackets. The

82

steepest part of the hillside is heavily wooded and more primitive with dirt rather than paved pathways.

In the center of the pleasing complex is an overlook with a low cement wall, three picnic tables and a fine view. Benches and trash cans are placed conveniently most everywhere. The entire area is protected by a chainlink fence on three sides.

A basketball court, playground and several group picnic areas occupy the west extremity. There's even a tiny-tot playground for those five years old and under.

This delightful city park is closed from sunset to sunrise and when it is open, dogs must be on a leash.

Above the group picnic area, one of the elegant lamp posts typical of Gerstle Park. This is the only botanical garden in Marin and is well worth visiting just to see the specimens of trees and plants.

PICKLEWEED PARK

—————————————————————————————33

places to play & long levee walks

WHERE KERNER AND Canal Streets meet in San Rafael you'll find Pickleweed Park, an expansive spread poised for your outdoor enjoyment.

Actually, there are three city parks — Pickleweed, Schoen and Shoreline — merged into an intriguing complex of space, in places bordered by the elegant Spinnacker Point townhouses. You'll find ample parking and room to bike, jog, run, amble, bird watch or just plain enjoy.

A scientifically planned Parcourse Fitness Circuit begins at a sandy playground with slides and sturdy structures for the kids. From there it leads to the canal proper and pretty well follows the levee. Each station has its exercise instructions and ratings depending upon your physical condition.

There are green lawns for picnicking, tables, shade trees, a splendid soccer field and a huge bricked facility for barbecuing. The Pickleweed Park Community Center building is comparatively new, attractive and is capable of handling a wide variety of events, seminars, gatherings and the like. For more information call 485-3077.

Bordering Pickleweed to the south is Schoen Park with its roofed picnic table, swings, slides, pine trees, benches, trash barrels and a drinking fountain. This also marks the beginning of Spinnaker Point Townhouse development on East Canal Street.

The levee is paved along here, instead of gravelled. Where Schoen Park terminates Shoreline begins. It's fine walking with many easy access routes, benches facing the canal, even a gazebo if you want to sit in a bit of elegance.

Townhouses blend in nicely and seem to befit the pleasant atmosphere. As you walk southward you'll pass even more fitness stations. Just prior to reaching No. 11 the pavement ends and so do the townhouses. You're on the levee in open space now, and it's a good feeling. There are indications of future development.

Even so, there will always be room here for outdoor enjoyment. All three parks are open sunrise to sunset.

Weeping willow and the elaborate playground structure at the beginning of Pickleweed Park. Playing fields and levee walks stretch toward the bay along the canal.

RESOURCE RECOVERY CENTER

34

pigs & geese part of plan

THIS IS A HUGE noisy facility. A sign on a wall inside one of the buildings reads, "Marin Recycling and Resource Recovery Association."

We didn't hear much on the tour. The docent was obviously well informed, but the racket of conveyor belts, fork lifts and the sound of glass, metal and wood being segregated, pulverized, smashed and reduced simultaneously blocked her out.

Still, my wife, Jayne, and I got the message: The one great hope to save open space, our resources and the environment is to recycle and reduce garbage. Half the garbage brought here and reduced, prior to being hauled to fast-diminishing dump sites, could be recycled. It's up to each of us to segregate even more at home first, then this efficient processing center can do the rest.

We learned that Marin is already a leader in that direction, thanks to Ted Wellman and Gloria Duncan who, back in the early 1970's, recognized the problem, and to Joe Garbarino, chairman of the facility, who got it underway and keeps it moving ahead.

A group of fourth graders were in the tour that day, and from what they saw and heard and the questions they asked, we knew they, too, left with greater awareness of the problem and hope for Marin and our planet.

But the tour didn't end there. Following our docent, we crossed the road and entered the resource's animal kingdom where more surprises were in store.

"Does anyone know why we have pigs here?" the docent asked.

"To eat garbage," a student responded.

"No," she said, "our 200 pigs don't eat garbage. Nor do our cows, sheep, goats, horses, chickens, ducks and geese. Pigs and the others are fed damaged bread, bruised produce, outdated dairy products and bakery goods, things that would otherwise have to be dumped by stores. They bring it here instead. Then once a year we auction off surplus animals. It works well."

Flying Can Ranch, Marin Recycling Center, Marin Sanitary Service and Marin Waste Reduction Facility are all located at the end of Jacoby Street off Bellam Boulevard in San Rafael where they combine their efforts to keep our county from becoming buried in garbage. A visit here is a real eye-opener.

Happy pigs snooze in the ooze at Flying Can Ranch across from the busy facility. More bucolic fields sport other animals who also do their part in recycling damaged food stuff.

SHORELINE STRIP ROCK WALL

look toward the bay & you're far away

D ID YOU EVER think a rock wall would be a good place for outdoor fun?

Well, there's one on San Pedro Road north of downtown San Rafael that offers a lot. When you crest the hill beyond Loch Lomond Harbor there it is, a nearly mile-long arc of piled rocks between Main Drive and the road leading to McNear brickyard, a sturdy breakwater capable of holding back San Pablo Bay's nastiest storms.

San Pedro Road is still divided at this location. Right away you'll discover a small park facing the bay with green patches of lawn, benches, shade trees, a paved pathway and even a drinking fountain. There's parking room at the curb for several cars. To walk the entire length of the path protected by rocks piled high is something of an adventure. At least, it's good exercise with a magnificent view of the Marin Islands to the east, wooded hills beyond the road to the west.

For some reason it never seems to be overcowded here, perhaps because most folks are headed for either Peacock Gap or McNear's Beach. The recent Saturday I visited this fascinating stretch of shoreline, the mini-park was empty with a few windsurfers out in choppy bay waters at the northern extremity.

Quite a number of bicyclists zipped past, a few joggers but for the most part I felt alone and in tune with nature, a rapture which had not been realized when driving by.

En route I passed several Golden Gate Transit bus stop signs which means you can escape by bus if you don't feel like driving.

Regardless, the rock wall can be an interesting and relaxing place for a picnic, hike, bicycle ride, or perhaps some jogging, running, or even windsurfing.

Fishing? You bet, but it's unlikely you'll ever find the rocks lined with anglers. This day there were none. But I do know a few who cast for striped bass with Wormtail Jigs when the tide is right, and they do well. Other species are also taken here by those in the know. It might just be worth a try.

At the start of a mile long rock wall, showing a patch of lawn and typical huge boulders. The tide is out and across the water you can see, nearby, McNear brickyard, and dimly in the distance, Contra Costa shoreline and hills.

SANTA MARGARITA VALLEY PARK

36

play, picnic or climb a hill

A SPECIAL SPOT in a hollow at the head of a valley surrounded by open space, Santa Margarita Valley Park is a well-designed compact complex operated by the City of San Rafael. Everything you need for fun, exercise or relaxation is here in this superb spot for kids. The sandy play area for tots boasts a yellow cement boat and a Loch Ness monster of the same color and material. Swing seats are replicas of little sea horses and there is a cave and tunnel to crawl through.

For older children, there is a sandy play area of space age climbing structures including a gyroscope, spiral slide and other ingenious, challenging creations resembling space vehicles.

A fine grassy knoll separates the playgrounds from tennis and basketball courts. Trails lead eastward up the hillside through scattered redwoods and pines to open space. There you'll find a mysterious semicircle of 20 pilings driven into the ground and standing two or three feet high, a few scorched from fire. Anti-errosion? A lookout spot? Whatever, they seem to belong there.

A trail leads west through coyote brush, oak and bay trees to a picnic area carved out of the hillside with three sturdy tables, screened by Portuguese laurels. The perimeter is marked by logs anchored on hefty stones and arranged to be used as rough benches.

Nearby a large fallen buckeye spans the dry creek which harbors huge boulders and the twisted trunks of laurel trees. On the downside toward the parking area, a small wooden bridge crosses the streambed to another picnic and barbecue space.

By now you've circled the park and are back by the restrooms, bike rack, drinking fountain, and the parking area, happy for the outdoor experience.

To locate Santa Margarita Valley Park, follow Freitas Parkway off 101 to Del Ganado, turn right, go to the end, left on De La Guerra Road for a short distance and you're there.

Above the semi-circle of short poles, looking down on the courts and playground. Picnic tables and the creek are off to the left.

SANTA VENETIA MARSH

37

encircling levees for grand exercising

POSTED METAL SIGNS state it well:

"Santa Venetia Marsh. Open for public use and enjoyment. Hiking, horseback riding, dogs on leash, bikes on protection roads, camping by permit." So this is an expanse for nature lovers, birders, joggers, health enthusiasts and the like.

My wife and I began our trek at Pump Station #4 off the short segement of Vendola Drive opposite the old school. We crossed a couple of new wooden foot bridges with sturdy railings and out onto the broad levee road to begin the loop. It was a cold, blustery day with billowy dark clouds and rain squalls that made for brisk walking. We stepped along, the only folks in sight, marvelling at the open space, the great stretch of marsh extending eastward to San Pablo Bay.

We were close to the point where Las Gallinas Creek enters the bay and were intrigued by the way the location is ringed by Marin's lovely hills from three sides — north, west and south.

This day was so clear we could even see the east bay hills dotted with silvery petroleum tanks in the distance near Rodeo.

Big yellow signs announced an underground pipeline crossing plus one across the slough reading, "Caution, 5 mph, weak levee."

Soon we arrived at Pumphouse #5 on another end of Vendola Drive. From there back to our starting point along the high levee, you're skirting the backyards of many homes, barbecuing equipment in evidence.

We noticed that nearly all east-west streets in the residential area end against the levee and have eight-stair accesses, with appropriate signs, leading up to it.

Back at the car we reflected on all we'd experienced on our invigorating big circle walk. And we gave thanks to the Marin County Open Space District for the preservation of this bit of "as was" to "as is," thereby making Marin a better place to live.

A bridge over the slough leads across the marshland on this invigorating walk. A wonderful spot to breathe salty air and look for birds.

SANTA MARGARITA ISLAND

38

wooded hump of land surrounded by water

A LITTLE GEM, Santa Margarita Island is scarcely a seagull-mile from Civic Center. There's not a lot of parking room at the end of Meadow Drive off North San Pedro Road but that's where the entrance is. On a weekday, you'll have no trouble.

A wide cement bridge, barricaded against vehicle traffic, crosses a slough to reach Santa Margarita on the south fork of Las Gallinas Creek.

The small intriguing island is open for public use and enjoyment. Hiking, running, jogging, horseback riding and bird-watching are allowed. Dogs must be leashed.

My wife and I chose to crest the wooded hill among numerous jagged outcroppings of rock. We ambled slowly beneath bay trees and gnarled old oaks with a scattering of madrone while observing and carefully stepping around that ever-present poison oak. In the green grass of almost-spring we saw miner's lettuce, milkmaid and brodiaea. Farther on we saw scattered toyon bushes.

There's a tortured old oak at the hilltop with a trunk hollowed by fire. To us it symbolized strength, endurance, defiance and a rugged beauty, scarred but gallantly alive.

Once down the other side we came to a broad path that surrounds the base of the island with many level picnicking spots. Across the slough

94

to the south and east are homes, docks and boats. From the west shore, the view of Civic Center is now nearly obliterated by the elegant homes of a new development. Mount Tamalpais and a broad sweep of marsh are still visible.

It was here we happened upon Marin County's one and only survey crew consisting of three members, all hard at work driving stakes or behind a transom.

"What's the purpose?" I asked.

"Too much silt and mud in the sloughs," one answered. "This is in preparation for dredging."

Following a pleasant exchange, we completed our maiden tour of Santa Margarita, and felt grateful to the county's Open Space District for preserving this enchanting little island so close to home. We'll be back.

The broad cement bridge crosses Las Gallinas Creek to the small wooded island. Path on the right leads around Santa Margarita, or you can go straight up by the boulders to the top.

JAKE'S ISLAND

39

salt marsh, muddy trail, up the hill

CRISP CLEAR WINTER days are great for exploring Marin's California State parks. We were on North San Pedro Road, giving China Camp the once over when we stumbled upon an exciting adventure that turned out to be Jake's Island.

Ever been there? You could slip by without noticing. There are no signs except a discrete one beside a wide gate proclaiming the area state property. Many small amenities have been added recently. The chained iron pipe gate is freshly painted, with a no dogs symbol adorning a sign. Beyond, where a broad road starts to skirt a wooded hill, there is an elaborate little structure with a peaked shingle roof, displaying a map of the area on one side, the birds you might see on the other. From this you learn names of the surrounding landmarks. That's Turtle Back, a great round oak-studded mound. The road hugs its base and nature trails climb its sides.

We came to newly installed signs, the first one about bunch grass, the next telling of the importance of salt marshes.

Half way around Turtle Back we saw a stretch of muddy road which crossed the marsh to Jake's Island. The sign about the island stated that it was named for Jake, reportedly a poacher and that the trail might be impassable at high tide. It almost was. Large puddles and gooey mud made the way difficult. But we weren't about to turn back when, just beyond, the road started climbing into Jake's oaks.

"Let's try skirting the puddles on the matted pickleweed," my wife suggested.

"I can see water beneath," I said.

"This stuff is springy. We won't sink. You go first and see."

She was right. Soon we were breathing the exhilerating air as we puffed up the incline, bare branches at roadside proclaiming the winter presence of our ubiquitous poison oak. At the crest of the hill we stood where there was evidence of an old homesite. Blooming narcissus and the shiny leaves of other planted bulbs marked the garden area. Fruit trees bloomed. Planted by a poacher? What a view from beneath the oaks! No wonder Jake, whatever he was, had settled here.

We found ourselves walking very slowly back to North San Pedro Road and our car, reluctant to end our intriguing adventure.

From the road skirting Turtle Rock, looking across the spongy marsh, the trail leading up into Jake's oaks is visible. Views from the other side of the island are grand.

SHORELINE TRAIL

40

fine easy trail & new access

CHINA CAMP STATE Park's 1690 acres has many attractions. Shoreline Trail is one of the most popular for nature lovers, joggers and hikers. This three mile stretch follows the contour of the hills above North San Pedro Road, and from the park's eastern boundary, meanders westward through woods and open space for three miles until reaching Miwok Meadows. Within that distance, be prepared for surprises and many unforgettable glimpses of ever enchanting San Pablo Bay.

Something new has been added to further enhance the route, and to offer an alternative for those choosing to use it. A new trail now begins near Weber Point and historic China Camp proper. The project was accomplished by the Marin Conservation Corps and funded in part by the California State Coastal Conservancy. This trail connects with Shoreline offering the choice to walk either east or west at the junction of the older path.

First, however, you must gain elevation, and to do so from Weber Point you cross North San Pedro Road where a new split rail fence marks the beginning. Here you will see some unusual work encompassing four switchbacks with retaining walls made of rocks and railroad ties, a noteworthy accomplishment in trail construction obviously built to endure.

This is a steep, heavily wooded hillside as the new trail zigzags upward to finally meet Shoreline. This day we chose to walk eastward where we broke out in a clearing near the crest of the ridge with China Camp below with its quaint old pier and Mount Diablo in Contra Costa County across the bay.

Taking the trail in the opposite direction before reaching Miwok Meadows, you'll catch glimpses of Weber and Buckeye points with their picnic tables and choice spots for relaxing. Birdlife is prevalent and chances are you'll see squirrels, deer and perhaps even a fox.

Plans are to extend Shoreline Trail the full length of the park connecting with Back Ranch Meadows. At open places you'll be able to view Jake's Island, Turtle Rock, their surrounding salt marshes and all that this intriguing area offers. Also planned are numerous loop trails to offer visitors more variety.

Newly constructed switchback trail, opposite Weber Point, climbs up to meet Shoreline, where you can go either way. This section was dedicated March 1991.

JERRY RUSSOM PARK

41

as it was years ago, it still is

A NICE SIGN, beside the simple but impressive cement and wood entrance, states in carved letters, "Jerry R. Russom Park, City of San Rafael."

The story behind the 180 acres of open space beyond that sign is quite inspiring. The late Jerry Russom and his neighbors living in the vicinity of Canyon Oak off Lucas Valley Road, knew the area belonged to developers.

"In the early 70's," said Marge Russom, Jerry's widow, "we approached the local homeowners association and expressed the opinion that perhaps the land could be bought, given to the city and dedicated to open space."

As it turned out, San Rafael paid half, the association the rest. A result of this joint effort is a precious spread of Marin saved in its original state which abuts other areas of open space.

Within this park, I walked old Lucas Valley Road from Canyon Oak west to Lassen Drive one morning. To my left as I started out, tawny oak-studded hills dipped to a large green playing field. On the right, I came upon a straight young tree dedicated to the memory of Fred Okey Jr., dated September 23, 1979. The creek meanders here under old twisted oaks and splendid laurels which shade a number of fine picnic spots.

A bit farther on the left a laurel grove with ferns covers a steep hillside. Old roads and trails branch south toward the ridge. It's easy walking along the flat with plenty of choices for more strenuous hiking up steep, adjacent terrain.

No motor driven vehicles are allowed here. During the whole round-trip stroll of perhaps a mile, I only saw one other person — a man walking his black dog on a leash.

I liked the primitive atmosphere. You won't find picnic tables and barbecue pits here. But if you're an outdoor enthusiast, you will find freedom, solitude and beauty, thanks to cooperative people with vision and foresight.

From HWY 101, take the Lucas Valley off-ramp to Canyon Oak Drive on the left. It's a short piece to the entrance with limited parking.

Entrance to Jerry Russom Park. Creek is off to the right and hill rises on the left. The old roadway leads a half-mile to hit new Lucas Valley Road. Trails to open space branch off along the way.

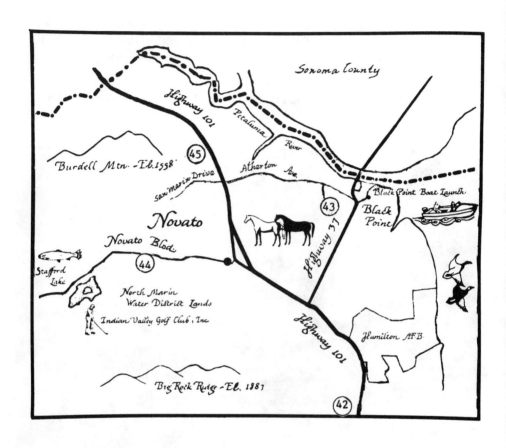

Sonoma County

Highway 101

Petaluma

River

Burdell Mtn. - El. 1558'

San Marin Drive

Atherton Ave.

(45)

Novato

Novato Blvd.

Stafford Lake

North Marin Water District Lands

Indian Valley Golf Club, Inc

(44)

(43)

Highway 37

Black Point Boat Launch

Black Point

Hamilton AFB

Highway 101

Big Rock Ridge - El. 1887

(42)

102

NORTHERN MARIN

MILLER CREEK PARK

—————————————————— 42

a gentle stroll beneath tall trees

T HE ENTRANCE WE took to this neighborhood park is graced by a
picnic table, drinking fountain, a series of sturdy swings for youngsters, a bench and sandbox, near the spot where Miller Creek
meanders beneath Las Gallinas Road north of San Rafael in Marinwood.
We parked just before the bridge.

Enchantment lies beyond but is well concealed by a screen of fine
old oak and California laurels as the path follows the creek from above on
the west bank. Keep your eye peeled for the old arched steel bridge to the
left. Chances are you'll hear happy voices echoing from a nearby school
playground. The scent of the forest is pleasing and a gray squirrel or two
will probably scamper from branch to branch in the spreading trees.

On the left, in a magnificent grove of trees, is an array of well spaced
picnic tables. A sign states that this is Marinwood Community Park open
6 a.m. to 11 p.m., dogs on a leash, no motor bikes. Such a cool, shady,
inviting spot, ideal for family gatherings or group picnicking.

Before reaching Miller Creek Road, where a strip of lawn designates
another entrance, the trail passes maintenance buildings and tennis
courts, veering away from the creek. On the lawn, you circle the courts,
then head back toward the creek. Perhaps here is a spot to pause beneath
a magnificent old oak where benches invite you to sit awhile.

Crossing the bridge, a cement one with wooden railings, gaze into
Miller Creek. You'll be struck with the amount of running water despite,
at this time, five dry winters. Notice the height of the water-carved banks:

104

You'll wish you could see it after a rousing rain storm. Now you have another chance to sit, this time beneath a scarred old bay tree.

Some of the trail is paved along here and leads directly to Miller Creek School grounds. Bear right on the dirt pathway and you'll skirt the school and end up back on Las Gallinas near the completely restored and relocated historic 100-year old school.

Now it's only a short walk north to where you left your car parked at the entrance by the swings, completing a gentle lovely one-half mile loop.

Interesting arched steel bridge over Miller Creek is only one of the many sights on this gentle walk in a neighbor-hood park.

DEER ISLAND

43

wonderful trails away from it all

I T'S NO LONGER an island but the deer don't seem to care.

One thing is certain. This is indeed a fascinating piece of Marin County open space preserved for public use and enjoyment. Ideal for hiking, jogging, bird-watching, horseback riding, walking your pet or just leisurely soaking up nature, Deer Island Loop is worthy of your attention. You can even camp here by special permit.

Counterclockwise seems the most popular approach from the limited parking area at the trailhead. It leads south up a gentle slope by an old cement-based root cellar. Oak-studded hills are on your left, a Ranger residence, then dilapidated farm buildings to your right. Gullies are crossed on broad-planked bridges. Quite suddenly you break into the open, over grassy knolls. Beyond to the southwest stretches the Novato flood plain, swampy acres during wet years, but given more to tules and grasses during droughts and dry seasons. Rowland Plaza can be seen far beyond.

Novato Creek meanders in the distance, finally worming its way toward the base of Deer Island proper. In spring a profusion of wildflowers adds a special rainbow of colors beneath the trees and in the clearings. California laurel and oaks mix closely to form a rather heavily wooded cover over the island. You'll see an occasional buckeye tree, a number of deadfalls and some last-leg moss-laden oaks.

Below the trail to the east with Highway 37 in the distance, are several ponds, part of the Novato Sanitary District. Now you've made at least three fourths of the loop, covered over two miles and have less than one back to your starting point.

Deer Island Loop came into the Marin County Open Space District in 1978, and consists of 135 acres. For more information call (415) 499-3687.

To get there from Highway 101 going either north or south, take the Atherton Avenue turnoff at Novato, head east 1.8 miles to Olive Avenue, turn right for .7 to Deer Island Lane. Turn left and drive a short distance to the small parking area on your right where the road swings around a complex of industrial buildings.

One of the wooded rocky knolls on Deer Island showing a clump of oak trees and the tan grasses of a dry season.

NEIL O'HAIR PARK

44

a creek runs through it

NEIL O'HAIR IS Novato's largest city park, 100 acres, and covers an expanse of land ideal for recreation including horseback riding, hiking, jogging, bird-watching, picnicking and trout fishing. A new open air, roofed shelter offers protection from the elements, if needed.

Turn south on Sutro Avenue where it begins opposite San Marin Drive off Novato Boulevard. Go just a short distance to the bridge which is near the park entrance on the right. There's parking space for eight or ten cars on the shoulder.

This is where Novato Creek is dammed summers to form a fine fishing hole thanks to the local Kiwanis Club that sponsored the project several years ago. Arrangements were made for the Department of Fish and Game to regularly stock the area with catchable rainbow trout, much to the delight of youngsters, particularly when school is out. The Morning Star Horse Farm to the north stands on 23 acres leased from the city, fulfilling the needs of those with equestrian interests.

Within the park, huge veteran oak trees invite you to spread a blanket and open a picnic basket beneath the protection of sturdy limbs that offer ample shade. Or you can meander along above the creek on various trails or on an old road that leads to a huge grassy meadow some distance beyond, fenced at the far end.

From there it's unspoiled scenery in all directions. You'll see thickets, home to a variety of birds and small animals, and in spring and summer, wildflowers adding a profusion of colors all along the route. There are patches of poison oak to sidestep but the going is easy most of the way, the creek always making music within hearing yet not always within sight.

To the south an old road skirts a ranch house, corrals and a pasture. Don't be surprised if two or three horses come toward the fence, nodding to be petted. Just beyond, on your left, a steep hill rises but is closed to public access. Stick to the road that meanders above the creek offering a variety of scents, sights and sounds — indeed a peaceful interlude. Future plans are for expansion to further enhance the location.

Above Novato Creek, a new structure adds to enjoyment of Neil O'Hair Park. This is near the entrance. Trails wind along the creek and an old dirt road leads to a wide meadow.

OLOMPALI PARK

ancient history comes back to life

C OAST MIWOK INDIANS had a propensity for choosing comfort, convenience and beauty for their villages.

The proof lies at Olompali State Historical Park which was opened to the public in October 1990, just west of Highway 101 north of Novato. As of this writing, many restorative improvements are scheduled, but no need to wait. The message is clear if you attend any time. This 700-plus acres of peaceful landscape contains more than you can digest in one visit.

A large parking area sets the tone for whatever leisurely endeavor you have in mind be it hiking, jogging, birding, picnicking, lazing or reflecting the historical significance of this fascinating area.

The central grounds are spacious and nearly flat with numerous picnic tables spread beneath magnificent old oaks, laurels and a wide variety of other trees, including tall, stately swaying palms. An impressive old fountain once spilled from a rocky island pinnacle into a large, oval cement pool, now fenced and dry with the promise that one day it will operate again.

You'll see many buildings of historical value and walk the cement stairs with stone ballistrades that lead down to remnants of the formal gardens from the original Burdell mansion built in 1911.

From at least 2000 BC Coast Miwoks lived here. Then, in 1846, this was the scene of the only casualties of California's famed Bear Flag Revolt.

You'll find plenty of room to roam and even explore trails leading west into steeper terrain, or meander through ancient walnut orchards with rock outcroppings typical of Marin evident on hillsides. Many more trails are planned for the future.

Olompali has belonged to the State of California since 1977. A dedicated organization called Olompali People have cooperated with the state to help preserve the location.

There is a $5 parking fee, $1 less for seniors. Dogs must be leashed and a $1 fee paid for each. No camping. The park is open from 8 a.m. to 5 p.m., but closed Tuesdays and Thursdays.

Part way up the trail, looking back down to the old barn. This state park is a fascinating piece of history in the process of being restored.

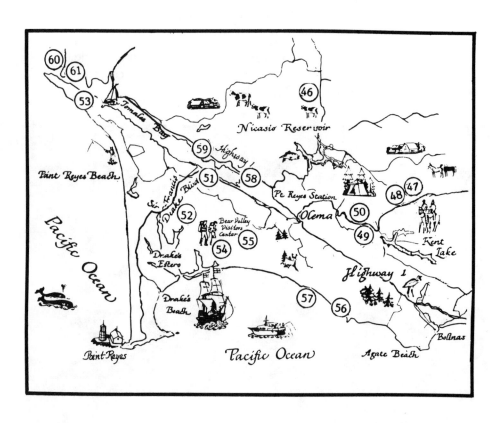

WEST MARIN

CHEESE FACTORY

46

a perfect place to picnic

THE CHEESE FACTORY on the Petaluma-Olema Road, is a splendid place to relax and enjoy a picnic lunch, take respite from the road or do some speciality cheese shopping.

There are many things here to make a family outing notable — fine lawns, spacious grounds, picnic tables, clean restrooms, ample parking on new, clearly-marked blacktop. There's even a group picnic area in a nearby pine grove. Most buildings are cream-colored, red-roofed, some old, some new, all involved with the manufacture of fine cheeses.

Inside the attractive store you'll find a variety of items besides cheese, the principal product — wines, breads, even T-shirts. There's an 1865 picture of the Cheese Factory's founder, Jefferson Thompson. His descendants (four generations of Thompsons have worked here) still run the Marin French Cheese Company at 7500 Red Hill Road, as they have for well over 100 years.

The spacious grounds are immaculate. You can see for miles, the rolling landscape featuring bald hills and canyons cloaked with oaks, laurel, buckeye and sometimes redwood and fir trees.

Folks come from miles around to sample Rouge et Noir Camembert and Brie cheeses. They are world famous because the Thompsons have continued to adhere to the historical French formula.

The Rouge et Noir factory also produces a breakfast and schloss cheese popular with visitors and have available many attractive gift assortments. Two weeks are required in advance of delivery date when ordering assortments. This gives the staff time to select the proper cheeses and to prepare for shipping.

The entire complex is fascinating, the atmosphere conducive to relaxation and the joy of sampling superb foods.

If you want to see the manufacturing process, you can. Tours are conducted every 30 minutes daily from 10 a.m. to 4 p.m.

Oh, yes. If your kids are under 16, there's a one acre pond there stocked with bluegill, catfish and black bass just for them. No license needed, a nice little added attraction.

The pond where youngsters can fish and ducks paddle on the placid water. Note two of the many picnic tables on the wide expanse of lawn.

ROY'S REDWOODS

through the meadow and into the woods

FOR YEARS WE'VE driven Nicasio Valley Road. Just beyond San Geronimo Golf Course, well below the road, we always glimpsed a wide beautiful meadow. It looked magical. Finally, one day we stopped. There's room to park on either shoulder: We took the downhill side. Marin County Open Space District's green, blue and white signs, with the pictoral do's and don'ts, were posted at fire road gates, and announced the site as Roy's Redwoods.

We chose to walk the trail on the east side of the road that meanders across that lovely long meadow surrounded by woods we'd viewed from above. A prominent redwood grove with huge trees caught our eye on the right. It's dark and mysterious in there with some deadfalls, but plenty of room for picnicking or meditating. The forest duff is spongy and warmly rust colored. There is little undergrowth with scattered patches of blackberries and ferns.

The monarchs of Roy's Redwoods are awesome, rising hundreds of feet skyward with sturdy, massive, even fire-scarred trunks.

Farther along the meadow gives way to a forest of tall young bay trees. Grassy knolls rise beyond, criss crossed by animal and walking trails. You'll traverse several rocky streambeds, alive with the cadence of moving freshets in wet seasons, signs of their activity clearly visible even when dry.

At the crest of one hill where the trails fork, we decided to return by a broader, well travelled horse trail that crossed a water course on a

116

sturdy plank bridge with railings. We were above the meadow now, winding along the hillside, slowly losing elevation. Below, at the edge of the meadow, we saw a watering trough and more of the location's beauty from a different perspective.

I became so intrigued with the 312 acres split by Nicasio Valley Road, I dug further and found that Thomas and James Roy owned the property for about 80 years beginning in 1877. They had a dairy ranch and operated a shingle mill at the foot of Nicasio Hill. Despite their lumber interests, they had great respect for the giant redwoods and made sure many were preserved. Thanks to Tom and Jim Roy, they still stand in all their awesome magnificence for our enjoyment.

A view of the long lush meadow ringed by Roy's redwoods. A trail leads into the woods straight ahead, through the bay trees and up the hillside where it meets other trails. This is a magical place.

MAURICE THORNER MEMORIAL

48

switchback trails, gnarled oaks, rugged cross

FOR THIS ADVENTURE, take Lagunitas School road off Sir Francis Drake Boulevard at San Geronimo, drive a half mile to a locked fire road iron gate on the left and a sign marking the entrance to Maurice Thorner Memorial, a 33-acre preserve. Parking is limited. The trail climbs steeply up the grassy slope, angles sharply in the opposite direction to start a series of switchbacks.

On this crisp overcast day, we found the climb particularly invigorating. The view below us began to unfold, the school and playground growing smaller, our vista of the wooded ridges beyond increasing in size and splendor.

Soon we entered the woods, a heavy growth of madrone, Douglas fir and oak with a scattering of ferns and, on fallen logs, patches of fungus. An unseen jay scolded us, then another. A bushy-tailed grey squirrel branch-hopped above, then scooted down one tree and up another. The woods smelled damp and refreshing.

As we approached the crest of the hill, nature's violence became evident by an increasing number of deadfalls and uprooted trees. Strong winds obviously are not strangers here.

We passed through a unique grove of gnarled old oaks defiantly reaching skyward, toughened by surviving years of storms. Then suddenly we stepped onto an open knoll, the trail riding the crest of the grassy ridge. Far beyond we could see a cross silhouetted against the gray windy sky. "I'm walking to it," I told my wife.

Perhaps a quarter mile beyond, it was an awesome sight rising rugged and strong at the highest point of a rounded hill. Once there, I stood dwarfed beneath the 14-foot cross, my eyes fixed upon spikes placed where Christ's hands and feet would have been.

Below me was Nicasio Valley Road and the San Geronimo golf course, the traffic on nearby Sir Francis Drake Boulevard barely audible. At last I looked away, vowing to return some Easter sunrise, and with the full understanding why Robert Thompson and Maurice Thorner deeded this beautiful site to the county. Thorner died before the dedication in 1981 so Thompson requested the parcel be named in his memory. The Board of Supervisors agreed. As I finally retraced my steps, I could see Jayne in the distance sitting on a rock, patiently waiting . . .

At the crest of the hill, one of the typical wind-stressed oaks leans, partially uprooted, but still survives. Mist almost obscures the next ridge.

PIONEER TREE TRAIL

49

a world of silence & towering redwoods

WITHIN THE BOUNDARIES of Samuel P. Taylor State Park, at the west end of the bike path bridge that crosses over Sir Francis Drake Boulevard, you'll find the beginning of Pioneer Tree Trail.

It parallels Lagunitas Creek upstream for a short spell then climbs away on switchbacks through redwood groves and scatterings of oak, bay, madrone and Douglas fir with rock outcroppings here and there. You will see a few large uprooted trees, impressive evidence of the forces nature periodically arouses. But the trail is broad and easy to walk as it gently gains elevation. In spring the forest floor is a profusion of white iris with sprinklings of other wildflowers.

Then you're in a world of silence punctuated only by the occasional sound of a bird or the rustle of a small animal. The trail curves around bluffs and in and out of small canyons, some with an abundance of ferns.

Suddenly it's there before you, a magnificent redwood, a patriarch of the forest. There's no sign to tell you it's the pioneer tree the trail is named after, but there's a conveniently placed bench nearby for you to rest a moment and reflect on the beauty of the spot, the straight young redwoods looking very much like sentinels standing guard around their grand master.

As the trail finally progresses into Wildcat Canyon and down along the creek to meet up with the bike path you left over two miles back, you'll see many fire-scarred giants. Some places wooden railings guard against the abrupt drop to the creek below.

Now that you're back on the paved bike path and within the sound of traffic along Sir Francis Drake Boulevard, it's a good time to use your imagination. You're headed east along the old North Pacific Coast narrow gauge railroad. Listen hard and you might hear a plucky little wood burning eight-wheeler chugging through the redwoods pulling a few warped coaches. The happy voices of long-ago picnickers might carry above the noises of the hard-working engine.

The reverie probably won't end until you reach your car and are headed homeward. Then you can reflect upon the fascinating loop you've taken, the escape, the endless wonders of nature.

The gentle trail, shaded by stately redwoods, leads past ferns and wildflowers as it climbs and dips in a quiet world.

DEVIL'S GULCH

50

exciting walk along a rambling creek

ANOTHER ATTRACTION WITHIN the boundaries of Samuel P. Taylor State Park is Devil's Gulch, a canyon well worth visiting.

A sign marks the entrance but if you're not careful you'll get by without seeing it. There's parking space on the west shoulder of Sir Francis Drake Boulevard for a half dozen or so cars.

A gate blocks vehicles from the narrow blacktopped road at the start. It's 100 yards to the trail that bears right along the creek. When my wife, Jayne, and I visited the gulch, we hiked the creekside trail all the way to Stairstep Falls, about 1-1/4 miles. The gulch is heavily wooded with twisty laurels, oaks and madrone, some uprooted from recent winds, others from the devastating storm several years ago. A few downed trees still block the trail. Uprooted bay trees, like redwoods, somehow manage to sprout anew and go on living.

Large ferns cover the steep-sided canyon. Jayne assigned me to the salmon watch while she, in a professional manner, fulfilled a photographer's role.

We soon came to a magnificent crawl-through redwood, a smaller version of a drive-through. We crossed a number of rustic plank bridges with sturdy rails, trod through a eucalyptus grove with nearby Douglas fir trees reaching for the sky.

We met an Asian couple toting a small child. "Half mile," he said grinning and pointing upstream, making signs like stairs with his hands.

122

We found Stairstep Falls to be more uniform than spectacular, but worth visiting. Hope when you walk the trail, the county is not experiencing a drought. Abundant water in the stream helps its beauty.

On the return trip Jayne snapped pictures of shiny scarlet mushrooms and the few wildflowers already blossoming here while I searched pools and riffles in vain for spawning silver salmon.

All too soon our mini-safari ended, but not without a warm feeling of contentment.

Through a tangle of trees, one small pond is visible in a stream quite low because of drought. However, even in dry conditions, it's a beautiful place.

CHICKEN RANCH BEACH

secluded, sheltered & right at hand

T HE FOLKS OF Inverness know where it is, cherish its handy location, and often choose to walk rather than drive there. For others traveling in either direction on Sir Francis Drake Boulevard, they will probably slip by without ever knowing.

We're talking about Chicken Ranch Beach. There are no signs and only limited parking on the shoulders of the boulevard. The beach is blocked from view by heavy roadside growth, yet on hot summer weekends, this short stretch of tawny, shell-fragmented sand reportedly plays host to up to two hundred guests.

We found a path opposite Pine Hill Drive leading through the trees which partially screened a portable latrine and several nearby trash cans. Later we even saw a doggy-do bucket and a pooper-scooper hanging on a post marked by a sign which pictured a canine. We crossed a small waterway on a wide plank and there we were on Chicken Ranch Beach. A picket fence formed the boundary at our left, a sandspit to our right with marshland beyond toward Barnaby's restaurant and Golden Hinde Motel. The tide was high, the scene enchanting with Marin's rolling hills clearly visible across Tomales Bay.

"What a great place to bring kids," my wife said. "No breakers, little current, a small, cozy beach."

A mother and two young children sat near the water's edge. One child contentedly munched a muffin, proudly displaying to us this prized goodie tightly clutched in a small fist.

"How is it when the tide's out?" I asked.

"Not as pretty," she replied with a grin. "Mud flats."

"Can you walk to Barnaby's along the shoreline?"

"It's possible at low tide. Swampy, though."

Soon another mother approached with two small boys. The lead fellow ran across the plank shouting, "My Chicken Ranch!"

The other, wearing rubber boots, chose to wade the creek. Too deep. His mother warned him just in time. He wanted to return home for higher boots.

We lingered, absorbing the unique solitude and seclusion, fully understanding the lack of signs. You really don't want to advertise such a delightful spot when it's so easy to reach.

Sitting on the warm sand at the water's edge, two small boys and their mother enjoy Chicken Ranch Beach. Across Tomales Bay, Marshall is visible, then the rolling hills of Marin.

MOUNT VISION

52

up up up for the view of views

I F YOU'RE DRIVING in West Marin in the vicinity of Inverness be sure to visit Mount Vision. Traveling west on Sir Francis Drake Boulevard, you'll see a sign 3.4 miles beyond Inverness. It's a curvy narrow blacktop road that gains altitude quickly as it winds through grove after grove of weather-stressed Bishop pine.

After about three miles you'll break out into the open with grassy hills sporting patches of coyote bush. Before you is a small but adequate parking area bordered by huge rocks. A large map standing under thick plastic, supported by an ample wood foundation, clearly illustrates and names many points of interest spread before you in a sweep of land and seascape of unbelievable proportions — Drake's Bay, Point Reyes, Ten Mile Beach, Chimney Rock and many more. On a clear day, you can see the Farallones.

The only thing that isn't clearly definable from this impressive vantage point is Mount Vision itself. You're obviously close to the summit, but the road curves onward and upward and soon you feel the pull of what lies beyond. Could it possibly offer more than this spot?

Behind the wheel again, you pass a small pond or two and other places to park for varied visions of Point Reyes National Seashore spread below, each underscoring a different and inspiring aspect, unobstructed scenery in nearly all directions.

A mile beyond the first stop Mount Vision Road is blocked by a locked iron gate. There's a large gravel parking area on your left marked by a rustic fence, and a magnificent view of Tomales Bay to the northeast. Heavily-wooded slopes lead up the mountain to where you stand in awe. This is a wildlife area so no dogs allowed. You can, however, continue on foot up Mount Vision Road which is still paved. A sign reads, Inverness Ridge Trail .5 mile with the same distance to the Bucklin Trail.

Once you can convince yourself it's time to leave, don't expect the descent to look the same as the climb. You'll notice different angles and pass many spots you won't recall. That's the wonder of Mount Vision Road — four miles up, four miles back for an enchanted eight mile drive.

Standing behind the huge boulders at Mount Vision's big lookout, you can see Drake's Bay and estero, with the tip of Point Reyes reaching out into the ocean. Ten Mile Beach is on the horizon toward the right.

TOMALES POINT

53

where tule elk roam again

F ASCINATING IS ONE word that applies to Tomales Point Wilder- ness Area. There are, of course, many other befitting descriptive adjectives. Most satisfying, however, is to visit and leisurely explore this exciting headlands peninsula which separates Tomales Bay from the Pacific Ocean.

The 3,000 acres are in West Marin at the end of Pierce Point Road. After leaving Inverness on Sir Francis Drake Boulevard heading for Point Reyes, bear right at the crest of the hill. Watch for clearly marked directional signs, drive just over nine miles on Pierce Point Road to the gravelled parking area facing the ocean beneath a row of stately, aged cypress trees and near a cluster of historic white dairy ranch buildings.

At the trailhead are signs and maps. It's 4.7 miles to Tomales Point, 3 miles to Lower Pierce Ranch site and Bird Rock Island on the Pacific side. The trail is broad, hugging the headlands. Far below a lively surf crashes relentlessly against a rugged, rocky coastline broken occasionally by a short, curved inaccesable beach at the mouth of a gully.

Suddenly the trail dips into a saddle, giving us a glimpse of Tomales Bay on our right, then reaches upward for the ridge. The spring day we took the hike was blustery and cool with buttercups, lupines, poppies and other wildflowers sprinkled in beddings of fresh green grass. Rocky outcroppings here and there added a certain enchantment to the wild, rolling landscape.

Then it happened. We spotted a herd of seven wary tule elk feeding on the ridge. They watched curiously as we approached for closeup pictures, then circled across the trail to feed on the Pacific side. Tule elk became extinct here years ago. Then in 1977, two bulls and eight cows were reintroduced and since the herd has grown. It was a rewarding experience to see these magnificent animals at such close range.

While here, you can also visit nearby McClure's Beach and tour Pierce Point Ranch's grounds with many wayside displays. Tomales Point is blessed with natural beauty and charm.

Seven stately tule elk amble slowly by on their way to graze above the ocean. Views from the ridge are extensive in all directions. We spent three hours hiking six miles and didn't see it all.

POINT REYES HOSTEL

54

haven for hikers, rustic retreat

T HE UNIQUE SIX-mile drive to Inverness Ridge and the Point Reyes American Youth Hostel holds lots of surprises. Giant old oaks are soon replaced by Douglas fir as the broad paved road curves its way upward, ducking in and out of little canyons, some thick with the growth of young fir trees.

You left Bear Valley Road near its junction with Sir Francis Drake Boulevard and are now headed up the Limantour Road to enjoy the fascinating hill country beyond. Just before you reach the ridge, on the left, is Sky Trailhead which leads southwest into the wilderness. There's ample parking. No pets, fires or bikes, camping by permit only.

Now, as the road rides the ridge, panoramic views open up on either side, rolling coastal hills and valleys leading seaward to the west. The road dips and swings with the natural curvature of the land. You pass Bayview Trailhead and an adjacent parking area on the right.

A mile or so beyond, an elegant Bishop pine on the left marks the entrance to an overlook where an illustrated map explains the existence of the trees native to the ridge. Below in a valley is Point Reyes Youth Hostel. Once back on the road, it dips sharply. At the bottom, turn right for Muddy Hollow, left for the hostel. Limantour Beach is two miles straight ahead.

It's just a short distance to the hostel, a cozy country complex of old ranch buildings nestled comfortably beside the road. It's a haven for nature lovers, hikers, bikers or those seeking a unique retreat and a different, gratifying experience, ideal for families or groups. You can stay in either the main ranch house or a bunkhouse.

The complex can house up to 44 guests and pre-paid reservations are required two or three weeks in advance. Rates are $8 per night per person, half price for children with parents. Bring your own food, soap, towels and sleeping bags. No alcohol allowed.

Phone (415) 663-8811 between 7:30 and 9:30 a.m., 4:40 and 9:30 p.m. for reservations and additional information.

Looking up at the main ranch house at Point Reyes Hostel from the road. It is well worth making necessary advance reservations to spend time here.

MOUNT WITTENBERG

55

vigorous hike to a great view

A S WITH TRAILS to many offbeat, remote and exciting locations, one rigorous route to Mount Wittenberg, highest point on Inverness Ridge, starts at Point Reyes Visitor Center off Bear Valley Road near Olema.

We parked our car at the farthest end of the wide area and started out on a crisp, overcast morning with full realization we have over thirteen hundred feet to climb to the summit in the relatively short distance of 1.6 miles. Sky Trail branches to the right just two-tenths of a mile from the starting point. A many-trunked ancient bearded bay tree and a sign mark the spot.

The steep beginning soon puts us into a dense forest of old- growth fir with a profusion of sword fern and low bushes. The trail is well-maintained and punctuated occasionally by shallow drainage trenches angling downward across the path. The degree of slope varies as we press ever upward, winding beneath mixed conifers. This morning the trail is deserted except for my wife and me.

We pause often to catch our breath and enjoy the solitude of the forest. Finally we break out into a sweeping green meadow. The trail flattens a bit, giving us a breathing spell, then resumes climbing through another meadow and by more rail fences.

Now it's steeper with some switchbacks bolstered by sturdy plank retaining walls. Log stairs assist us at intervals. Then we break out into the open, the trail ahead reaching for Inverness Ridge in a direct manner, taxing our weary legs even further. At last we reach a crossing of trails where signs designate locations and distances in several directions. The breathtaking view is, unfortunately, obscured by haze and mist.

The summit of Mount Wittenberg is still two-tenths of a mile straight up a pronounced incline. No use quitting now.

At last we look down at a United States Department of Interior circular brass survey marker. A scarred sign nearby simply states: Mount Wittenberg, 1407 feet.

We return by Meadow Trail, a longer more gentle descent, easier on our wind, harder on our knees! We arrive back at the car just past noon. Our vigorous adventure consumed three and one-half wondrous hours.

This is looking back up a piece of our downward path on Meadow Trail where trees meet overhead and ferns grace the banks.

POINT REYES BIRD OBSERVATORY

56

a place to study feathered friends

ON THE WINDSWEPT northern Marin Headlands, Point Reyes Bird Observatory offers much to those who love birds and the outdoors.

Adjacent to Point Reyes National Seashore, you get there by taking the Olema-Bolinas Road and turning right on Mesa Road prior to entering the town of Bolinas. Watch for signs.

Drive four miles, past the Coast Guard transmitting site on your left with all its skyhigh wires and antennas. There's a reassuring road sign here that says Point Reyes Bird Observatory, .5 mile. This last half mile is curvy gravelled road.

At the dirt parking area you'll see a sign reading, "A non-profit research station dedicated to the study and conservation of birds."

Low brown nearly flat-roofed wooden buildings are surrounded by bent trees and coyote brush. The visitor's room is small but impressive. There's a large stuffed pelican and an owl to greet you. Six glass display cases tell and show a lot. Illustrated display boards outline the observatory's objectives in research, conservation and education. Centered in the small room in a glass enclosure is a relief map of the southeast Farallon Islands.

This research area is a great place to explore and enjoy. You definitely get the feeling that those working here love what they're doing and believe in the goals of the observatory.

Pamphlets are available, most of them free, some with a clearly marked fee. The room is open from 7:30 a.m. to 5 p.m. daily, with bird banding as specified on a large board where handwritten messages tell when the next banding will be and invite you to join in. It's an informal, friendly little place with classrooms and bathrooms to the rear and even a picnic table and badminton net just outside.

There were few people about the recent Thursday my wife, Jayne, and I visited. This is a spot you go to on purpose unless you happen to be lost on the mesa. At any rate, you'll find it worth the visit. Those working there will make you feel welcome and you're bound to learn at least a few interesting facts.

The modest building that houses Point Reyes Bird Observatory, nestled on a flat above nearby bluffs that drop to the ocean. This is a working place and you're welcome to drop in to watch, to help, to learn.

PALOMARIN BEACH

steep trail, sheer cliffs, tidepools

MESA ROAD OFF Olema-Bolinas Road is only four and one-half miles long but leads to many interesting places in the short distance before it deadends. Once our car had climbed through a dense forest of old growth eucalyptus, we broke out onto a high plain, passed a fire station on the right, the road to Agate Beach on our left. Eventually, RCA's impressive complex of poles and wires and related radio equipment came into view on the left.

Beyond, the road turns to gravel and winds downward by a ranch and finally to a sign that announces the entrance to the Point Reyes Bird Observatory.

A bit farther, the road ends in a large dirt parking area against Palomarin Trailhead, a starting point to explore on foot the headlands to the north.

We opted to drive back a short distance to a smaller gravelled clearing for cars. This is where a steep and twisty half-mile trail threads its way down to a long strip of gray pebbles that points northward and hugs the base of almost vertical bluffs.

"So that's Palomarin Beach," I said. "Heard a lot about it."

"Yes," Jayne replied. "Hope I can make it back up."

We stopped to read a sign warning against gathering and eating mussels from May 1 to October 31.

Quickly descending, we pass a young eucalyptus grove on the right, then approach an overlook marked by a podium which displays an

136

illustration of tidepool exploring, what to look for, how to enjoy the adventure, and the dangers to be aware of.

As the trail wiggles steeply downward, we pass several protective railings, each a chance to pause and look below at the Pacific Ocean crashing against the jagged coastline.

At last, the trail cuts into a small canyon and finally slides onto the pebbled beach. What solitude!

But all too quickly the afternoon wanes and it's time to gird ourselves for the steep climb out. We walk slowly, stopping again at each overlook to catch our breath and to search out points of interest we may have missed during our descent.

Part way down the steep half-mile trail, the curved dark sand beach, precipitious cliffs and tidepools are visible. The great solitude on this beach is worth the climb.

TOMALES BAY TRAILHEAD

58

bucolic scenes, reservoirs and old railbeds

ONE MILE NORTH of Point Reyes Station on HWY 1, slow the car down and keep glancing to your left. Within a half mile you'll see the entrance to a gravelled twenty car parking area and a sign announcing "Tomales Bay Trailhead," a recent addition to the National Park Service.

A designated wildlife area, this location is of particular interest to birders, naturalists and those who enjoy strolling gently rolling hills with interesting rock outcroppings here and there. Camping is prohibited and no pets or horses allowed.

A narrow zig-zag entrance leads through a fence and onto a trail that crosses a gully and bears west on what was once a farm road. Geologists and historians have always been drawn here; there's much to attract the attention of both. As the trail slopes gently toward the very head of Tomales Bay, a flood plain stretches before you. Far beyond, on the other side, heavily wooded hills swoop steeply upward to Inverness Ridge, peaking at Mount Wittenberg, and farther west, Mount Vision.

Closer at hand you see a small reservoir to the left of the trail and a herd of about fifty cows grazing peacefully on a grassy, rounded hill. The animals scarcely give you a curious glance as you walk cautiously past. Beware of the poison oak.

Now you're in full view of the head of Tomales Bay as it stretches northward toward the open ocean. Hugging the shore and sometimes crossing open marshland is what looks like an old road. Here's where historians perk up, for they recognize the remnants of another century — the roadbed of the old North Pacific Coast narrow gauge railroad that ran from Sausalito to Cazadero carrying Russian River bound vacationers and hauling lumber back from the prime redwood forests near Duncan Mills.

Once again, it's easy to stand in the silence on the bluff above the marsh and envision that diamond-stacked eight-wheeler pulling weathered coaches of happy passengers and hear, as the train rumbles by over trestles, the engine's high-pitched whistle announcing its presence in lilting, nostalgic tones.

The author, dwarfed by an outcropping of rock, waves to the photographer. Inverness Ridge is across Tomales Bay. The trail leads to a bluff that drops to the marshland where the trains once ran.

MILLERTON POINT & SIEROTY BEACH

59

two spots in one where ospreys nest

FIVE MILES NORTH of Point Reyes Station on HWY 1, look to your
left for the entrance to Millerton Point and Alan Sieroty Beach. A
tall, aged mixture of eucalyptus and cypress trees marks the spot.
Swing into a gravelled parking area faced by more tall trees. Both of the
adjoining facilities are under the umbrella of Tomales Bay State Park.

It's shady here, and sometimes windy, but nonetheless inviting.
There's one picnic table and barbecue grill back against some protective
willows. Nearby is a convenient unisex facility with handicap access and
beyond a trash dumpster.

Westward and to the left, a wooden bridge crosses a small gully
enroute to Sieroty Beach. Again on your left, a trail leads to a pair of
secluded picnic tables with a barbecue grill standing ready. In spring the
pathway to the beach is bordered with tall grass, poppies, filagree, wild
sweetpeas and other growth.

The beach is a one-half mile gentle arc of tan, shell-flecked sand
reaching to Millerton Point. Inverness is clearly visible on the opposite
shore.

Should you choose to follow the railed fence from the parking lot
that leads over a grassy knoll to join the beach about half way to Millerton
Point, it's an easy pleasant alternative. And you get to study a posted
explanation concerning ospreys. There's a utility pole beyond the fence
topped, between March and July, by an active pair of nesting osprey.

140

These are fish-eating hawk-like birds that breed in this area during those months prior to wintering in Mexico. The female usually hatches one or two hungry chicks. But here in the 1960's, osprey were threatened to extinction by pesticide contaminants. However, these birds have staged a rather impressive comeback since the banning of DDT. The count from near zero has blossomed to about 18 nests along Inverness Ridge alone.

Visitors to Millerton Point and Alan Sieroty Beach are asked to please stay behind the railed fences and not to approach the utility pole topped by the osprey nest. This sanctuary is the result of a combined effort by PG&E, Santa Cruz Predatory Bird Research Center and the California State Park System.

Showing the dirt path, grassy bluffs, and huge driftwood trees. Two men exchange words on the beach that curves to Millerton Point. Inverness is directly across the bay.

DILLON BEACH

quaint village, engaging surf

A S DILLON BEACH is one of the northernmost spots in Marin County, perhaps you've never visited. Those who have undoubtedly would rather keep it a secret, but there's no way. The five-mile drive from the town of Tomales after leaving State Route One, is curvy and intriguing, working its way seaward in delightful fashion over rolling hills with unusual rock outcroppings, some insignificant, others so pronounced as to automatically cause unscheduled photo stops.

The approach to the seaside community with many hillside homes of various architectual styles remains hidden until the road bursts out of a canyon and there you are, still above the sea, surrounded by multi-windowed houses with porches, some elaborate, others more conservative, many with terraced gardens. On the right, you'll notice an unusual retaining wall constructed of sandbags.

The downtown portion of the community seems rather undefined in a pleasing manner, the various shops befitting the casual atmosphere that is predominate. Suddenly the road turns sharp left and there before you is a magnificent view of the broad beach below, a vast panorama of surf laced with lines of breakers. Far beyond, across the bay, is Tomales Point dipping sharply to the ocean with Bird Rock just around the point.

The invigorating scent of salt-tinged air is as refreshing as spring. This is where Tomales Bay meets the sea, and does so in an unforgettable manner. The road decends to beach level and there, in front of you, is a sandy expanse of magnificent proportions dotted with drive-to picnic tables and barbecue grills. The beach is private and there's a five dollar per day parking fee. No dogs, but a splendid location for family barbecues and outings with children.

Beyond the toll booth guarding the beach, the road heads southward up a rise with sand dunes all around. Now you're driving in front of a row of cottages and beach homes facing the sea, each with its own private view. Soon you know that just a mile beyond is Lawson's Landing famed for its clam barges and wonderful camping facilities, but that's another story . . .

Cars on the sand-blown parking lot, next to the barbecue tables. On the wide beach, various sports take place. Then there are the breakers and across the way, Tomales Point.

LAWSON'S LANDING

— 61

spacious camping, protective dunes

THE SIGN AT the toll booth lists your options and there are many ranging from a $5 entrance fee to a $180 monthly camping rate. You can rent a boat, launch your own, go ocean salmon fishing on either of two sturdy party boats or take the clam barge on minus tides for some exciting digging. Call ahead for reservations (707) 878-2443.

There's something inviting and intriguing about the broad grassy plain that stretches before you with sand dunes rising on either side. RV's are backed against dunes and thereby protected from the stronger sea breezes. Trails lead between sandy mounds to beaches and the ocean beyond. Picnic tables, latrines and dumpsters are strategically placed on either side of the road. Cattle graze peacefully in unoccupied areas.

Beyond, the road forks, left heading for breakwater campsites, right into an expansive complex of permanently planted trailer homes, ranging in age from vintage to contemporary. And then we're looking at a quaint store with a fine old sign reaffirming our location as Lawson's Landing.

Tall poles with protective tires mark boat lanes and a pier extends a short distance into the bay. This is where Tomales Bay meets the sea, a popular place with every convenience for campers, birders, anglers, crab fishermen and clam diggers.

Gravel roads crisscross around and through the complex in a casual manner. A few old commercial salmon trolling boats rest on land, some on aged trailers, testifying to life here in earlier times. We saw youngsters dipping crab nets or fishing off the pier. The store is well equipped to supply campers and anglers with their wants and needs. The salt-tinged atmosphere is conducive to slow-paced living and total relaxation.

We drove to the end of the breakwater and occupied the very last picnic table, enchanted by birdlife in the marsh beyond, the broad expanse of open bay and the hills to the west sheltering this location from the open sea. Such a delightful spot. "Peaceful waters," I muse. "Great camping spot. On such a day, this has everything — Marin at its best."

The pier at Lawson's Landing. This can be a busy place on a summer weekend, and wonderfully crisp on a winter day. Camping spots line the breakwater to the left. To the right, sand spits lead out to the ocean.

Spring pond, Neil O'Hair Park, Novato

— FURTHER READING ON MARIN —

Arrigoni, Patricia: MAKING THE MOST OF MARIN: A Best Selling Guide to the Most Stunning County on the California Coast, photography by author, Travel Publishers International, revised 1990 edition, — 5-1/2 × 8-1/2, 340 pages, additional historic photographs, maps. New sections on horseback riding and trails, lodging, transportation and entertainment. Complete coverage and accurate text make this a perfect reference book.

Dunham, Tacy: DISCOVER MARIN STATE PARKS, HIKING WEST MARIN, MARIN HEADLANDS TRAIL GUIDE, NATURE WALKS & EASY HIKES, WANDERING MARIN TRAILS, MARIN BIKE PATHS, SUNDAY OUTINGS IN MARIN, Cottonwood Press, 1987-'88-'89, — a delightful series of small 5-1/2 × 8-1/2 50-page books, illustrated by Troy Dunham with detailed maps and line drawings, and pertinent information well presented.

Fairley, Lincoln: MOUNT TAMALPAIS, A HISTORY. Picture editor, James Haig, Scottwall Associates, 1987, — 8-1/2 × 11, 202 pages, photographs, maps, fascinating and comprehensive text.

Golden Gate National Recreation Area: PARK GUIDE, published by Golden Gate National Park Association, 1990, — 4-1/2 × 10, 96 pages, black & white and full color photographs and drawings, maps, index, wonderful guide giving historical, botanical, geographical, ecological and recreational facts about this fascinating area. Pages 52-92, North of the Golden Gate.

Mason, Jack: THE MAKING OF MARIN, in collaboration with Helen Van Cleave Park, North Shore Books, 1975, — 5-1/2 × 8-1/2, 218 pages, historical photographs, maps, index. The first county history since 1880, this book is a treasure trove and well-worth searching for, a necessary addition to any Marinite's library.

Murdock, Dick: POINT BONITA TO POINT REYES, OUTDOORS IN MARIN, 61 PLACES TO VISIT, photographs and captions, Jayne Murdock, May-Murdock Publications, 1989, second printing 1992, — 6×9, 160 pages, maps, photographs of each place, index. Winner of Outdoor Writers Association of California's 1990 Best Book Award. Preface by William Filante, Foreword by Beth Ashley. Great book for planning over a year's worth of outings.

Spitz, Barry: TAMALPAIS TRAILS, maps by Dewey Livingston, Potrero Meadow Publishing, 1990 — 6 × 9, 312 pages, 12-page section of black and white photographs, appendix, chronological history. This marvelous book should be the close companion of anyone who ever sets foot on Mount Tamalpais. Well designed and beautifully written, it contains everything you need to know. Wonderful for rainy winter browsing to lay groundwork for your fair weather hiking.

Old Tocaloma Bridge

INDEX OF PLACES

BEACHES

Chicken Ranch Beach	124
Dillon Beach	142
Kirby Cove	20
Muir Beach	24
Palomarin Beach	136
Rodeo Beach	22
Schoonmaker Point Marina	38
Sieroty Beach	140

BICYCLE PATHS

Blackie's Pasture	52
Bothin Marsh	40
Pickleweed Park	84
Ross to COM	66
Walk to Alto Tunnel	44

CAMPSITES

Kirby Cove	20
Lawson's Landing	144
PanToll Ranger Station	32
Steep Ravine Campground	36

EDUCATIONAL

Slide Ranch	28
Resource Recovery Center	86
Point Reyes Bird Observatory	134

FISHING

Cheese Factory (pond for kids)	114
Elephant Rock	56
Kirby Cove (surf)	20
Lawson's Landing (charter boat)	144
Lime Point	18
Muir Beach (surf)	24
Neil O'Hair Park (creek for kids)	108
Palomarin Beach (surf)	136
Shoreline Strip Rockwall	88

OPEN SPACE

Bothin Marsh	40
Deer Island	106
Roy's Redwoods	116
Santa Margarita Island	94
Santa Venetia Marsh	92
(Maurice) Thorner Memorial	118

PARKS

Gerstle Memorial Park	82
Bayfront Park	42
Lineal Park	54
Boyle Park	46
Dunphy Park	38
Marinship Park	38
Miller Creek Park	104
Neil O'Hair Park	108
Old Mill Park	48
Olompali State Historical Park	110
Pickleweed Park	84
Robson Harrington Park	72
Sorich Ranch Park	76

PICNIC and/or BARBECUE AREAS

Albert Park	80
Bootjack	30
Boyle Park	46
Cheese Factory	114
Creekside Park	64
Dillon Beach	142
Dolliver Park	60
Dunphy Park	38
Gerstle Memorial Park	82
Bayfront Park	42
Kirby Cove	20
Lime Point	18
Miller Creek Park	104
Muir Beach	24
Muir Beach Overlook	26
Neil O'Hair Park	108
Old Mill Park	48
Olompali State Historical Park	110
PanToll Ranger Station	32
Robson Harrington Park	72
Rodeo Beach	22
Santa Margarita Valley Park	90
Sorich Ranch Park	76

PLAYING FIELDS

Albert Park	80
Boyle Park	46
Bayfront Park	42
Pickleweed Park	84
San Anselmo Memorial Park	74

PLAYGROUNDS

Albert Park	80
Boyle Park	46
Creekside Park	64
Dolliver Park	60
Gerstle Park	82
Lineal Park	54
Miller Creek Park	104
Old Mill Park	48
Robson Harrington Park	72
San Anselmo Memorial Park	74
Santa Margarita Valley Park	90

TENNIS COURTS

Albert Park	80
Boyle Park	46
Gerstle Park	82
Marinship Park (Sausalito Parks)	38
San Anselmo Memorial Park	74
Santa Margarita Valley Park	90

TRAILS

Baldy	68
Bootjack	30
Cascade Falls	50
Dawn Falls	62
Deer Island	106
Devil's Gulch	122
Faude Park	78
Jake's Island	96
Kirby Cove	20
Millerton Point	140
Mount Wittenburg	132
Olompali State Historical Park	110
Palomarin Beach	136
PanToll Ranger Station	32

Pilot Knob	70
Roy's Redwoods	116
Santa Margarita Island	94
Shoreline Trail, China Camp	98
Sorich Ranch Park	76
Steep Ravine	34
(Maurice) Thorner Memorial	118
Tomales Bay Trailhead	138
Tomales Point	128

VISTA & VIEWS

Baldy	68
Faude Park	78
Mount Vision	126
Mount Wittenburg	132
Muir Beach Overlook	26
Pilot Knob Trail	70

WALKS

Bothin Marsh	40
Lime Point	18
Lineal Park	54
Miller Creek Park	104
Neil O'Hair Park	108
Pickleweed Park	84
Ross to COM	66
(Jerry) Russom Park	100
Santa Venetia Marsh	92
Shoreline Strip Rockwall	88
Walk to Alto Tunnel	44

WATERFALLS

Cascade	50
Dawn Falls (seasonal)	62
Steep Ravine	34

Cascade Falls walk, Mill Valley

ABOUT THE MURDOCKS

Dick Murdock, born in Oakland May 15, 1917, lived in Contra Costa county most of his adult life, working for Southern Pacific out of Oakland. Five years — 1951-1955 — were spent in Dunsmuir, near Mount Shasta, on steam engines, as chronicled in his classic book, *Smoke in the Canyon*.

In 1972, his eyes and heart turned toward Marin. It was then that he fell in love with life-long Ross resident, Jayne Rattray May, divorced mother of five. Jayne, a trained journalist, was then teaching grade school in Mill Valley, living in the Ross home her parents had built in 1924 when she was only five.

They married there at a garden ceremony during the drought in February 1977. Already Dick and Jayne had pooled their impressive talents to produce his first book, *Walnut Creek's Unique Old Station*. Now they formed a small publishing company, MAY-MURDOCK PUBLICATIONS. Though both still held demanding full-time jobs, in that year they published two books, *Port Costa 1879-1941* and *Love Lines*, excerpted from their years of courtship correspondence.

Dick retired from Southern Pacific after 37 years in engine service on Memorial Day 1978; Jayne left teaching after 15 years in the summer of 1980.

So what does 'retired' mean to this pair? Total involvement in numerous projects, organizations, activities and publications that keep them busier than ever. In search of stories and relaxation, they try to break away one week a month for travel in their Adventurewagen, a goal seldom reached.

Lime Point to Lawson's Landing — 61 MORE Places to Visit, is their fifteenth book. It joins *Point Bonita to Point Reyes - 61 Places to Visit,* which the Murdock's published in 1989, as a perfect companion — both to the earlier book and to those readers who use it to explore Marin's fabulous outdoors.

Point Bonita, incidentally, received the first place BEST BOOK award from the Outdoor Writers Association of California at their 1990 summer conference, an honor the Murdocks revel in.

Dick's weekly columns in the *Marin Independent Journal* and monthly writings in the *Port Costa News* are constant deadlines which he works around the production of books or vice versa.

He and Jayne lead seminars throughout the Bay Area on such varied subjects as railroading, fishing and publishing.

The Murdocks are a true team doing everything on the books they publish except typesetting and actual printing. They serve as editor and critic of others' works and Jayne does most of the photography and design. In December 1990, a second computer was added to their workroom. Jayne felt it okay to ask Dick for time on the first computer to write a letter but when she wanted to produce a whole book (which she's working on now), she thought they better get a second computer just for her. She loves it.

Publishing books, gathering information for columns, doing outdoor research, getting away for mini-vacations in their Adventurewagen, and keeping up with their ever-expanding family (14 grandchildren between them — and four great-grandkids for Dick!) fills to overflowing their time.

Several books are in the planning stage, sitting patiently on the back burner, rail excursions are scheduled, plans made well into the next year. And the next!

ACKNOWLEDGEMENTS

To those who checked the manuscript for current accuracy and did incidental proofreading: Ron Stevens, Superintendent, Marin County Park and Open Space; John Dell Osso, Point Reyes National Seashore; John Martini, Golden Gate National Recreation Area. To Jean Guthrie for final proofing.

To those who provided maps for clarification and help: Laurence Dito, Director, Novato Parks & Recreation; Ron Miska, Marin County Parks & Recreation.

To Jill Thomas, at R. Nolan & Sons, who, with David Nolan, worked so hard to get it just right. We appreciate such dedication.

To Wayne Lowrence, Automagic Systems, who was always ready to talk us through any computer complexities without making us feel stupid.

To all others who answered questions, shared special knowledge and steered us in the right direction, we give thanks.

COLOPHON

Typesetting: R. Nolan & Sons, 4460 Redwood HWY, San Rafael, CA
using MagnaType on IBM PCs, translated with Blueberry
Software, Qume laser proofs, final output Agfa 8400.

Typeface: Text, Garamond light; Headings, Avante Garde Demi;
Initial caps, Avant Garde, Book.

Paper: 60# Glatfelter Thor white, recycled.

Printing & binding: Thomson-Shore, Inc. 7300 West Joy Road, Dexter MI

Color separation: Image Arts, 919 Filley Street, Lansing, MI

MAY-MURDOCK PUBLICATIONS
Drawer 1346 - 90 Glenwood Avenue
Ross CA 94957-1346 - (415) 454-1771

RAILROAD BOOKS BY DICK MURDOCK

SMOKE IN THE CANYON: My Steam Days in Dunsmuir

144 pages, 63 historical photographs,   hard cover $26.00

original artwork by Charles Endom   perfect bound   16.00

PORT COSTA 1879-1941: A Saga of Sails, Sacks and Rails

40 pages, historical photographs,

original artwork by Charles Endom   saddle stitched   6.00

HOGHEADS & HIGHBALLS: Railroad Lore and Humor

64 pages, sketches by Charles Endom   perfect bound   5.00

LOVE AFFAIR WITH STEAM

40 pages,   saddle stitched   3.00

EARLY CALL FOR THE PERISHABLES, A Day at the Throttle

24 pages,   saddle stitched   2.00

WALNUT CREEK'S UNIQUE OLD STATION

24 pages, 17 photographs   saddle stitched   2.00

BOOKS BY JAYNE MURDOCK

I PAINTED ON A BRIGHT RED MOUTH: The War Years

December 1941-August 1945

64 pages, vintage photo-collages   perfect bound   5.00

UNTIL DEATH AND AFTER: How To Live With A Dying Intimate

64 pages   perfect bound   4.00

BRIEF INFINITY: A Love Story in Haiku

64 pages   perfect bound   4.00

LOVE LINES: A True Love Story in Lyric Prose

by Jayne May & Dick Murdock, 134 pages   perfect bound   5.00

OTHER OFFERINGS BY MAY-MURDOCK

POINT BONITA TO POINT REYES: OUTDOORS IN MARIN
      61 Places to visit
      160 pages, 70 black & white photographs   perfect bound   10.00

SHANNON: WHAT'S IT ALL MEAN? 101 Commentaries
      by Wayne Shannon, 128 pages   perfect bound   6.00

THE NORTHWESTERNER — Twice yearly slick magazine of
      the Northwestern Pacific Railroad Historical
      Society, vintage photos, articles by well-known
      railroad writers.
      PREMIERE ISSUE, 1987, 24 pages: WINTER
      1987-88, 28 pages: SPRING 1988, 28 pages:
      FALL 1988, 32 pages: SPRING 1989, 32 pages:
      GOLD SPIKE ISSUE, FALL 1989, 56 pages: SPRING
      1990, 32 pages   each issue   5.00

SEND FOR FREE BROCHURE
MONEY BACK GUARANTEE ON ALL MAY-MURDOCK PUBLICATIONS

Levee Walk, San Rafael

Shoreline Trail, China Camp

Map by Dewey Livingston